Tai Shan

Hsi an (Chang an)

Huai — river w/out a proper mouth

Fen River   Peiching = Peking

WuTai Shan
Szu Chuan (large province)
   Chengtu

Image and Reality
in World Politics

北
Pei
North

西 West
   Hsi

East
Tung 東

South
Nan
南

Hu = Lake   Tung Ting ⟩ 2 of the largest lake
                    Po yang
Ho ⎫
or ⎬ river
He ⎭

Chiang = a big river

Shan = mountain

Ching = capital

Image and Reality
in World Politics

EDITED BY

JOHN C. FARRELL AND ASA P. SMITH

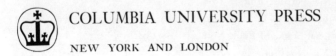

COLUMBIA UNIVERSITY PRESS

NEW YORK AND LONDON

To REINHOLD NIEBUHR, *who accepted "the wise man's task"
and has performed it to the benefit of us all*

Foreword

"Appearances to the mind are of four kinds. Things either are what they appear to be; or they neither are, nor appear to be; or they are and do not appear to be; or they are not, and yet appear to be. Rightly to aim in all these is the wise man's task."

EPICTETUS, *Discourses*

The gap between appearance and reality, which has been a staple of philosophers and literary men from Plato to Pirandello, has increasingly engaged the attention of students of international politics. Articles have been appearing in academic journals under titles bearing words like "perception," "misperception," and "image." And the eclectic discipline of international relations has borrowed some new concepts (and some new jargon) from the social-psychological approaches favored by many of the scholars who are studying the images held by decision-makers and the men in the mass who compose the nations they represent. "Cognitive dissonance" poses no immediate threat to balance of power as a central concept of the field, but it nevertheless must be included among the hodgepodge of conceptual tools with which scholars are patiently trying to fashion a comprehensive theory of international relations.

It might be wondered what took them so long to focus on this elusive realm of image and reality that has so long intrigued philosophers, poets, and playwrights. The importance of distorted images as a cause of hostility between nations is obvious to any American who has ever compared a

Chinese Communist description of the United States to the place where he lives. And any amateur student of history, reflecting on the causes of war, cannot fail to be struck by the role of distorted images and misperceptions in compounding the objective conflicts of interest that are ever present between nations.

This element of blurred subjectivity is a feature of all social conflict, not merely of that between nation-states. The American Civil War provides a classic example. One does not have to side with the revisionist interpretation of the causes of the war, which denies that there was a clash of interests making for an "irrepressible conflict," to conclude that it was precipitated by images that did not square with reality. Revisionist historians of the war overstate their case that the sectional, cultural, and economic divisions between an industrial, progressive North and an agrarian, reactionary South were not crucial, or that the moral issue of slavery was a fiction trumped up in the perfervid minds of abolitionist firebrands. But the reality of these "underlying causes" notwithstanding, the onset of actual hostilities was characterized by an unreality similar to that surrounding the outbreak of World War I, which Robert North and his associates have analyzed so closely. This unreality had its foundation in the caricatured images that were held in either section of the other, which assumed their most grotesque proportions with the election of Lincoln. It was perhaps best manifested by the extreme overreaction of the Southern leadership to the largely imaginary threat that the election of a "Black Republican" was thought to pose. Indeed, their behavior during the secession crisis would seem to substantiate one of North's most interesting hypotheses, which he elaborates in this issue: "Perception of one's own inferior capability, if anxiety, fear, or perception of threat or injury are great enough, will fail to deter a nation from going to war."

Historians, without concerning themselves with systematic analysis of the phenomenon, often allude to distorted images and misperceptions as part of their causal explanations for wars, as in the case of the Civil War. This is especially true of those who adhere to R. G. Collingwood's description of their proper task: "penetrating to the thought of the agents whose acts they are studying." But even most of those who do not follow Collingwood's philosophical idealism see man as the prime actor in the tragicomedy of human history. And this inevitably leads to a concern with man's views, from his *Weltanschauung* to his less elevated images and opinions.

This perspective was not shared by the political scientists who were in the vanguard of the developing discipline of international relations, most of whom focused on the abstract entity of the state, which they saw acting and reacting, more or less predictably, to objective forces and events in the international arena. This "billiard ball" model, as Arnold Wolfers has dubbed it, and its extremely deterministic philosophical underpinnings began to give way with attempts to develop a more comprehensive theory of international relations that would include the capricious human variable. Social scientists in the field began to see the utility of the historian's focus on human actors, while of course rejecting his insistence on the uniqueness of the actors and their historical situation in an effort to develop theoretical generalizations.

This "man-centered" research has been spearheaded by scholars interested in decision-making theory and in social-psychological approaches to the study of international relations. Much of it has come from the two leading research centers of the recently established scholarly industry of "peace research": the University of Michigan's Center for the Study of Conflict Resolution and Stanford University's Studies in International Conflict and Integration. Unlike earlier efforts in this vein that tended to attribute international conflict and war exclusively to man's psychological aberrations and irrational behavior, this recent research has been characterized by an acceptance of the truth of Rousseau's observation that the anarchical condition of the state system and the inevitable conflicts of interest which it generates are enough by themselves—without madmen or malefactors—to condemn its members to a "state of war." It has reflected an awareness that there can be no purely psychological theory of war or international relations, that there can only be psychological factors within a general theory. It has recognized that the relevance of the human actors and their motivations and perceptions is limited by the roles they play (and the constraints imposed by those roles) in the larger societal process and, moreover, by such givens of the international system as the distribution of power, the geographical location and international position of the state, economic conditions, and demography.

Although much of the work on images that is expressly theoretical in intent is being done by scholars using behaviorist techniques (four of them —Kenneth Boulding, Ole Holsti, Robert North, and Ralph White—included in this book), interest in the subject is by no means restricted to them. John Stoessinger, for one, is deeply interested in the theoretical implications of the gap between images and reality. Skeptical of behaviorism, he approaches the problem using the classical method, which Arnold Wolfers has aptly defined as the art of "mustering all the evidence that history, personal experience, introspection, common sense, and the gift of logical reasoning put at one's disposal." Moreover, beyond the purely

Foreword

theoretical considerations, the phenomenon of conflicting images of reality provides a useful point of departure for analyzing diplomatic disputes, as Stanley Hoffmann's article on Franco-American relations brilliantly demonstrates. Statesman and scholar alike can gain insights from considering difficult or hostile diplomatic relations in this context.

In the latter respect *Image and Reality in World Politics* is practically relevant as well as theoretically interesting. Each article points up the need to consider the subjective dimension in international conflict, to understand how and why the images held in other nations may differ from our own, and to make our images more realistic and our perceptions keener by eliminating the blinders imposed by nationalism, ideology, and rigid and hackneyed thinking. As the articles by Benjamin Schwartz, Stoessinger, and White suggest, part of this operation involves a simple act of empathy, and they show how important this act is in understanding our current conflict in Asia. However, seeing the world as others see it is an easy matter compared to seeing it as it really is. (Not the least of the difficulties are the complex and irresolvable philosophical questions concerning "reality" that the articles in this book necessarily beg.) Reinhold Niebuhr, Kenneth Boulding, and Ole Holsti point out some of the problems faced by men and governments in the effort to make their images jibe with reality: man's proclivity for myths and stereotypes, the built-in obtuseness of governmental hierarchies, and the cognitive processes that tend to sustain stereotyped images.

Holsti provides a common-sense prescription for overcoming these problems in his admonition to resist "reducing complexities to simplicities, ruling out alternative sources of information and evaluation, and closing off to scrutiny and consideration competing views of reality." A conscious and concerted effort to follow that prescription should make the "pictures in our heads" bear closer resemblance to reality, a requisite for a wise foreign policy as well as for survival in the present age.

Contents

Image and Reality
in World Politics

KENNETH E. BOULDING

The Learning and Reality-Testing
Process in the International System

The Aztecs apparently believed that the corn on which their civilization
depended would not grow unless there were human sacrifices. What seems
to us an absurd belief caused thousands of people to be sacrificed each
year. The arguments by which the Aztecs rationalized this image of the
world have largely been lost, thanks to the zeal of the Spanish conquerors.
One can, however, venture upon an imaginative reconstruction. The fact
that the corn did grow was probably considered solid evidence for such a
view; and in those years when the harvest was bad, it was doubtless argued
that the gods were angry because the sacrifices had been insufficient. A
little greater military effort would result, a few more hearts would be torn
from their quivering bodies, and the following year it was highly probable
that the harvest would be better and the image consequently confirmed.
Not only empirical evidence would support the doctrine, however; the
great truth that it represented could easily be held to be self-evident. The
seed must die if the corn is to grow. We all know, furthermore, that the
spectacle of violent death arouses the seed in man and is likely to produce

Kenneth E. Boulding is a professor of economics at the University of Michigan. His
published works include a dozen books and many articles over a wide range of fields,
including most notably in addition to economics the field of peace research and international systems. Among his recent books are *The Image, Conflict and Defense*, and
The Meaning of the Twentieth Century. From its beginning, he has been associated
with the Center for Research on Conflict Resolution at the University of Michigan.

an increase in the population. What could be more reasonable, therefore, than to assume that these two phenomena are connected?

If this is a parody, it is too close to the truth to be wholly comfortable. Arguments of this kind have often been used to justify human sacrifice and the image of the world that demands it, whether on the part of a religion or on the part of a state. The sponsors of the Inquisition thought that by roasting some people alive they would save many souls from roasting after death. The proposition that South Vietnam is a domino that has to be propped up by the dropping of napalm, the burning of villages, the torture of prisoners, and the sacrifice of American blood is a proposition that appeals to us much more strongly than these others; but it is being tested in much the same way as the Aztecs and the inquisitors tested their views of the world: by appeals to analogy, to self-evidence, and to the principle that if at first you don't succeed try more of the same until you do.

Image and Reality

The problem of what constitutes realism in our image of the world has bothered philosophers from the very beginnings of human thought, and it is certainly far from being resolved. Indeed, Hume may well have demonstrated that it cannot be resolved, simply because images can only be compared with other images and never with reality. Nevertheless, common sense leads us to reject Humean skepticism in practice; we must live and act for the most part as if our images of the world were true. Moreover, there are processes for the detection and elimination of error; so that even though truth constantly eludes us, by the progressive and systematic elimination of error, that is, false images, we may hope that we may gradually approximate it.

The elimination of error is accomplished mainly by feedback. From our image of the world we derive an expectation, that is, an image of the future. As time goes on, the future becomes present and then past. It is then possible to compare our image of the future with our image of the same period when it has become the past. In January we recall our image of December as we had it in November, and we compare this with our image of December as we have it in January. If the images do not correspond, we are disappointed and hence act to adjust one image or the other. There are actually three adjustments that can be made. We can adjust our image of the past and say that it was mistaken, that what apparently happened did not really happen and that we have been misinformed. We can adjust our past image of the future; that is, we can say that the image of December that we had in November was wrong. We can do this for two reasons, for our image of the future is derived by inference from our general view of the world. We can therefore say, on the one hand, that the inference was wrong and that our view of the world did not really imply that December should have turned out the way we expected; or, if we cannot deny the validity of the inference, then we must revise our general image of the world. The elimination of error can take place at all three of these levels.

The elimination of error, however, is only one of the results that disappointment can produce. Error exists primarily in our general image of the world. Disappointment, unfortunately, does not always force a revision in this image, for it can cause us to deny either the image of the past or the inference that gave rise to the image of the future. If a genuine learning process—the continual elimination of error in our image of the world, as well as the enlargement of this image—is to take place, there must be safeguards against rejecting inferences or rejecting the image of the past.

There are two levels of human learning-processes at which these conditions for the progressive elimination of error are met. One is the process of folk learning in everyday life, in which we learn about the immediate world around us and the physical, biological, and social systems that constitute our direct and immediate environment. Here feedback tends to be rapid; the images of the immediate past are especially hard to reject; and, because we are operating with fairly simple systems, the inferences that we draw from our general view of the world are likewise hard to reject. Consequently, disappointment causes us to make revisions in our general image of the world, and if these revisions result in further disappointments they will be further revised until disappointment is reduced to a tolerable level. People who are incapable of responding in this way to the feedbacks of ordinary life eventually find themselves in mental hospitals. Indeed, what we ordinarily think of as mental disease is the inability to perform reality-testing—the progressive elimination of error—on the folk-learning level. If a person's image of the world is entirely self-justified and self-evident, he will soon get into serious trouble. Suppose, for instance, that he is a paranoid and thinks that everybody hates him. All his experience will confirm this image no matter what the experience is. Experience that fails to confirm the image will be dismissed as due to either false inferences or mistaken images of the past. His fundamental image of the world is unshakable by any event that seems to contradict it. Such a person is incapable of learning, and it is this incapacity that really constitutes mental disease.

The other field where error is progressively eliminated and a genuine learning process takes place is in the subculture of science. Contrary to common belief, the method of science does not differ essentially from the method of folk learning. Both proceed through disappointment. (Indeed, it is only through failure that we ever really learn anything new, for success always tends to confirm our existing images.) Both methods are safe-guarded against denials of the image of the past, that is, of experience, and against the denial of inferences; hence in both cases experience that does not jibe with an image prompts modifications in the image. The only difference between folk learning and scientific learning is in the degree of complexity of the systems that are involved in each image of the world. Science deals with complex systems and folk learning with simple systems; but the methods by which errors are eliminated are essentially the same. Because of the complexity of the systems with which science deals, how-ever, it must use refined instruments and precise means of measurement in the development of its image of the past. It must likewise use highly refined methods of inference, employing mathematical and logical methods in order to derive its expectations of the future from its image of the world. It is in the refinement of perception and inference, however, not in the essential nature of the learning process, that science distinguishes itself from ordinary folk-learning.

We may perhaps illustrate the difference with reference to our image of space. The folk image of the world is that of a flat earth encased in the dome of the sky. For the ordinary business of life this image is quite adequate, and as long as we confine our movements to our immediate neighborhood it gets us into no trouble. Over a range of ten miles the curvature of the earth is quite irrelevant to the activities of ordinary life; and although the hills and valleys of the surface are much more relevant, we can learn about them through the ordinary processes of folk learning. For an astronaut, however, it would be quite disastrous to take an image derived from folk experience and to generalize it to the world as a whole. An astronaut requires the scientific image of a spherical—indeed, pear-shaped—earth. He must have very refined instruments and means of measurement. He must, at the very least, live in a Newtonian world and be capable of Newtonian inference, and as speeds increase he may even have to make Einsteinian adjustments. The folk image here would lead to immediate and total disaster. Nevertheless, this highly refined image of space has been obtained in ways that differ only in degree of sophistication from the methods by which we derive our image of how to get from our home to the post office.

The Literary Image and the International System

Between the world of folk learning and the folk images derived from it, and the world of scientific learning and the scientific images derived from it, there lies another world of images that I have elsewhere described,[1] perhaps unkindly, as the world of literary images. It is in this world that reality-testing is least effective and that the elimination of error either does not take place at all or is enormously costly. It is precisely in this world, however, that we find the images of the international system by which its decision-makers are largely governed, and it is for this reason that the international system is by far the most pathological and costly segment of the total social system, or sociosphere, as it is sometimes called. If we look at the various elements of the social system that are ordinarily regarded as pathological, such as crime, mental and physical disease, and economic stagnation, the international system probably costs about as much as all these put together, with the possible exception of economic stagnation, which is itself in part a function of the nature of the international system.

The direct cost of the international system must now amount to something like 150 billion dollars a year. This would include the total spent by all the nations on their military establishments, information systems, foreign offices, diplomatic corps, and so on. In addition, some estimate of the present value of possible future destruction should be included. Any figure placed on this is at best a wild guess. To be pessimistic, let us suppose that the destruction of a third world war would amount to half the present physical capital of the world, or about two thousand billion dollars, and that the chance of this happening is about five per cent in any one year; in this case we should add a kind of depreciation or discounting factor to existing world wealth of about 100 billion dollars a year. This would represent, as it were, an insurance premium for war destruction. A more optimistic assumption of, say, a one per cent chance of a major world war would reduce this to 20 billion annually. It is interesting to note, incidentally, that the size of the current expenditure on the war industry is almost certainly much larger than any reasonable insurance premium for war destruction would be. This points up a general principle that the cost of the war industry for any country in terms of resources withdrawn from the civilian economy is much larger than any insurance premium that might be conceived for a policy covering destruction by enemy forces. This is often true even in time of war. A study of the impact of the war

[1] Kenneth E. Boulding, *The Image* (Ann Arbor: University of Michigan Press, 1956).

industry on the Japanese economy[2] suggests that even during the Second World War the cost of the Japanese war industry to the Japanese economy was of the same order of magnitude as the destruction by the American war machine. One's friends, in other words, generally do more damage than one's enemies.

If we suppose that the gross world product is roughly 1,500 billion dollars, the international system and the war industry account for about ten per cent of this. It would be extremely surprising if all the other pathological elements in the social system taken together account for more than this. Crime and disease are likely to account for no more than five per cent of it, or 75 billion dollars. Even if we include the potential loss resulting from the failure of economic development, and if we suppose that a projected annual growth rate of two per cent is not realized, this would only amount to a loss of 30 billion dollars a year, as a measure of what might be called the pathology of the world economy. Even if we raised this projection to an optimistic four per cent, the loss would only be 60 billion, far below the cost of the international system.

One may object, of course, that it is unfair to regard the cost of the international system as if it were not offset by benefits, even if it is very hard to put a dollar value on them. We get the benefits of nationality: tangible ones like protection when we go abroad, and intangible ones like the sense of identity that thrills to the flag, that expands beyond the narrow limits of family and locality, and that responds gladly to the call for self-sacrifice. The sense of satisfaction that comes from being American or German or British or whatever is certainly an important benefit, however hard it is to evaluate. It must be recognized, however, that such advantages of nationality are virtually the only advantages of the nation-state system. There are no economic payoffs to the present system; indeed, in addition to the loss of resources we should also add the cost of tariffs and trade restrictions, and of the almost universally deleterious effects on the rate of development caused by high military expenditures. There was a time, perhaps, when the international system paid off for its principal beneficiaries, the great powers, in terms of the economic exploitation of their colonial empires. Even if the international system produced little gain for the world as a whole, it could be argued that it redistributed the world product in favor of those who played the international game successfully and became great powers. Today even this argument has little validity. Empire in the last 100 years has turned out to be a burden rather than an

[2] Kenneth E. Boulding (with Alan Gleason), "War as an Investment: The Strange Case of Japan," *Peace Research Society (International) Papers*, Vol. III, 1965, pp. 1-17.

asset. And in terms of the rate of economic growth, being a great power has not paid off. The British and French growth rates, for instance, from 1860 on were considerably less than those of many less ambitious countries, such as Sweden or even Japan. The German and Japanese attempts to become great powers were enormously costly; but their ultimate failure provides an even more striking insight into the realities of the present international system. After total military defeat and a complete loss of their great-power status, they have both achieved absolutely unprecedented rates of economic growth, far exceeding the growth rates of the victors.

This is indeed a strange world, in which nothing fails like success and nothing succeeds like defeat, in which great powers find that their greatness impoverishes them, and in which the way to get rich is to stay home and mind one's own business well and to participate as little as possible in the international system. Of course there are also historical examples of countries for whom defeat has been disastrous, though such examples are rather scarce since Carthage, or perhaps Byzantium. It is also possible to find examples of countries that stayed home and minded their own business badly. Such examples, however, do not affect the fundamental proposition that at least since 1860, when the impact of the scientific revolution on economic life really began to be felt, we have been living in a world that is qualitatively different from that of the past, a world in which, as I have said elsewhere, one can extract ten dollars from nature for every dollar one can exploit out of man. The scientific revolution, therefore, has completely eliminated any economic payoffs that might have been available through the international system in the past. And while diminishing the system's returns, the scientific revolution has at the same time enormously increased the cost of the system. In order to justify the continuation of this costly and precarious system, we have to put an enormous value on the nation-state as such and on the national identity it confers on the individual. It should at least be asked whether the value of these things is commensurate with the risks and costs of maintaining the system.

The Pathological State of the International System

What, then, are the sources of this pathological state of the international system? A number of answers can be given. Most significantly, a system of unilateral national defense, which still characterizes the international system in spite of the small beginnings of world political organization, is a "prisoner's dilemma" system:[3] the dynamics of the system produce an

[3] Anatol Rapoport and Albert M. Chammah, *Prisoner's Dilemma: A Study in Conflict and Cooperation* (Ann Arbor: University of Michigan Press, 1965).

equilibrium in which everybody is much worse off than in some alternative state of the system. In the two-country version of this system, let us suppose that each country has two choices: disarm or arm. They will clearly be better off economically and more secure politically if they both disarm. If both are disarmed, however, it pays one to arm—at least it may in terms of his image of the system. And if one is armed, the other will have a powerful incentive to follow suit. Both will probably end up by being armed, in which case both will be worse off than they would have been had they remained disarmed.

Whether there is an equilibrium in the world war-industry depends largely on the reactions of the parties concerned. The fundamental parameter here is the "reactivity coefficient," that is, the extent to which one country will increase its arms expenditures for each additional dollar that it perceives being spent on arms in another country. I have shown in another paper[4] that in a two-country system the product of the reactivity coefficients must be less than one if there is to be an equilibrium; otherwise the war industry will expand explosively until the system breaks down as the result of war or of some sort of parametric change. It can also be shown that the more parties there are in the system, the smaller the reactivity coefficient must be if an equilibrium is to be attained. It must certainly average less than one. As a reactivity coefficient of one might be regarded as normal, it is clear that a system of this kind must be abnormally unreactive if it is to achieve an equilibrium. It is not surprising, therefore, in the light of existing reactivity coefficients, which are certainly close to one if not above it, that the world war-industry maintains an uneasy and continually upward-groping equilibrium at about 140 billion dollars per year. Furthermore, this equilibrium, even if it exists, is inherently precarious in that a very slight change in the reactivity coefficients even on the part of a single country can destroy the equilibrium altogether.

The reactivity coefficients are themselves functions of the value systems of the decision-makers and of their general image of the international system, or perhaps of their images of other people's reactivity. And all these in turn are related to the gathering and processing of the information on which the decision-makers depend. The pathology of the international system, therefore, is closely related to the method by which it generates and processes information and the way in which these information inputs influence the decision-makers' images of the world. The question as to what is meant by the "reality" of these images in the international system is a

[4] Kenneth E. Boulding, "The Parameters of Politics," *University of Illinois Bulletin* (July 15, 1966), pp. 1-21.

very difficult one. In the first place, insofar as the system itself is determined by the decisions of a relatively small number of decision-makers it inevitably contains a considerable random element. The image of the system, therefore, should always be an image of probabilities rather than certainties. There is no very good way, however, of finding out what the probabilities of the system are. We do not have enough cases to compute frequencies like the life tables of insurance companies, and whenever one hears the expression "a calculated risk" in international politics one tends to interpret this as meaning "I really don't have the slightest notion." The epistemological problem itself, in the case of international systems, is very difficult; and one certainly cannot come up with any perfect solution for the problem of producing truth in the image of the system, for the system itself consists in considerable part of the images about it.

Even if the truth in an absolute sense may elude us, this still does not prevent us from discussing health, or at least disease, and there are certain diseases of the information system (and the images it produces) in the international sytem that can be diagnosed. The basic problem, as I have suggested earlier, is that adequate images of the international system cannot be derived from folk learning, because the simple feedbacks of the folk-learning process are quite inadequate to deal with the enormous complexities of the international system. At the present time, however, the role of science is extremely limited, indeed, almost nonexistent. We do not apply scientific techniques of information gathering and processing, even those available in the social sciences, to the image-creating processes of the international system. Social science, indeed, is regarded with considerable suspicion by most of the professional practitioners in the international system, perhaps rightly so, for it represents a certain threat to their status and power. On the whole, therefore, the images of the international system in the minds of its decision-makers are derived by a process that I have described as "literary"—a melange of narrative history, memories of past events, stories and conversations, etc., plus an enormous amount of usually ill-digested and carelessly collected current information. When we add to this the fact that the system produces strong hates, loves, loyalties, disloyalties, and so on, it would be surprising if any images were formed that even remotely resembled the most loosely defined realities of the case.

Almost every principle we have learned about scientific information gathering, processing, and reality-testing is violated by the processes of the international system. Indeed, the conflict of values between the subculture of science and the subculture of the international system may well turn out to be one of the most fundamental conflicts of our age. In science secrecy is abhorrent and veracity is the highest virtue. In science there is only one mortal sin: telling a deliberate lie. In the international system, on the other hand, secrecy is paramount and veracity is subordinated to the national interest. The national interest can indeed be said to legitimate almost every conceivable form of evil: there is not one of the seven deadly sins that is not made into a virtue by the international system. Another fundamental characteristic of the scientific community is that it is basically a community of equals, for the very good reason that hierarchy always corrupts communication. A dialogue can only exist between equals. In a hierarchy there is an inescapable tendency toward pleasing the superior, and hence confirming his own ideas. Hierarchy in organizations, therefore, produces a condition akin to paranoia in individuals. The information-gathering apparatus always tends to confirm the existing image of the top decision-makers, no matter what it is. This organizational "mental illness" is nowhere better illustrated than in the international system, which is composed of numerous foreign-office and military-establishment hierarchies that thrive on self-justifying images.

Finally, in the scientific community power is supposed to have a low value and truth the highest value, whereas in the international system the reverse is the case. It is not surprising that under these circumstances the international system is so spectacularly pathological in an organizational sense. Indeed, if one were designing an organization to produce pathological results, one could hardly do better than an information system dependent mainly on spies and diplomats. This is not to say, of course, that the individuals who occupy these roles in the international system are themselves necessarily crazy, although they do suffer from certain occupational diseases. On the whole, the people who run the international system are well above average in intelligence and education and even in personal morality, for they would probably not be content to serve in a system so absurd if they did not possess high moral ideals. Economic man does not go into the international system. He can live a better life outside it. It is the moral, patriotic, and self-sacrificing individuals who are most likely to be the active participants in the international system. It is the organization, not the individuals, which is pathological, by reason of the corruption of both the information and the values that have produced it.

Can the System Be Cured?

The next question, therefore, is whether we can learn to change the organization in ways that will make the whole system less pathological. There seem to be two general answers to this question. One is given by the advocates of world government, who feel that the defects of the present international system cannot be remedied and that therefore the only solution is to abolish it by transferring the locus of sovereignty from independent states to a world government. It is argued that this is a logical extension of the ongoing process in which smaller states have been absorbed or federated into larger ones, and that we have now reached the point where the existing international system is so dangerous and so costly that the sacrifice of national sovereignty sacrifices nothing but the dangers and costs. Only world government, it is argued, can prevent war or establish anything that even remotely resembles justice.

A somewhat less drastic view holds that stable peace is possible within the framework of an international system, given certain conditions, and that therefore world government in the strict sense is unnecessary. It is argued, in effect, that the pathological character of the international system which is so striking today is not necessary, but is rather a function of certain parameters and characteristics of the system, and that a non-pathological, healthy international system is conceivable and possible. Such a rehabilitated system, it is felt, might be more desirable in many ways than a unified world government.

These two approaches may not be as contradictory as they seem at first sight, though they do represent, in effect, two different solutions to the problem of the prisoner's dilemma, which, as we have seen, is at the root of the pathology of the international system. One solution to the prisoner's-dilemma problem is to change the payoffs of the game through the inter-vention of some third party. This is in effect what law, especially in its penal aspect, is supposed to do. The prisoner's dilemma in a sense governs all forms of the social contract, where each party has the choice of being either "good" or "bad." If they are all good, they will all be better off; and yet if they are all good it may pay one of them to be bad, in which case it pays all of them to be bad and they all end up worse off. The function of law and of government, in its role as the creator and sustainer of law, is that of altering the payoffs for the individual decision-maker so that it will not pay him to be bad even if everybody else is good. The business of government, then, is to define what is "bad" and to see that this kind of behavior is appropriately penalized so that the social contract is not broken.

The other approach to the problem of the prisoner's dilemma is the development of farsightedness on the part of the players themselves. This involves a learning process, and as Anatol Rapoport's experiments have suggested,[5] many people do learn after a while that "bad behavior" does

[5] Anatol Rapoport, *op. cit.*

not pay off in the long run. Hence they refrain from trying to gain temporary advantages that unilateral bad behavior might give them.

In the long-run development of the international system, both these processes may be observed. On the one hand, we have seen the development of supranational political institutions of slowly increasing capacity: the Concert of Europe, the League of Nations, and the United Nations. Each catastrophe apparently teaches mankind to set up institutions that might have prevented it, though they usually do not prevent the next catastrophe. Just as the generals are always supposed to be prepared to fight the last war, so the international institutions are designed to prevent it. The slow learning process nevertheless goes on, and the institutions themselves can be regarded as repositories of political skill and knowledge. Indeed, for the meagre resources that we devote to the international order, we get a remarkable return. This becomes apparent when we consider that the combined budget for all the international agencies is less than that of the Ford Foundation.

Along with this process of developing world political institutions, we have also seen the development of areas of stable peace within the international system even without supranational institutions. The two best examples are probably North America and Scandinavia, though the socialist camp may be another example and perhaps by this time all of Europe, although it is a bit early to say. Stable peace, at any rate, is a recognizable phase of the international system, which tends to pass into this phase when a certain level of maturity in national behavior has been reached. One might even suppose, perhaps a bit optimistically, that relations between the United States and the Soviet Union might develop as they have between the United States and Canada or among the Scandinavian countries.

The growth of stable peace requires a learning process on the part of the national decision-makers, a learning process that includes the accumulation of tradition and role images which are passed on from role occupant to role occupant. The process involves a change in values as well as in actual images of the system, and these are closely related in a very intricate and complex manner. The nation-state can no longer be treated as a sacred institution; there must be a deflation of the emotions and values that attach to it, a decline, if you will, in the passion with which people love their countries and an acceptance of the nation-state and the nation-state system as essentially mundane institutions designed solely for public convenience.

One great problem that the world is likely to face in this connection is that the maturation process of the nation-state takes place at different rates, so that at any one time some are much more mature than others. This, however, may give the immature ones an advantage, since they will be able to elicit more passionate devotion to the national cause from their citizens. This is perhaps one of the most persuasive reasons why the mature states, who have outgrown the adolescent disease of nationalism, should be all the more concerned to set up world political institutions that have some hope of exercising restraint on the less mature states. What might be called the "mature-conflict-behavior solution" of the prisoner's dilemma depends on both parties being mature. If only one party is mature, then a third-party alteration of the payoffs is the only solution, which in this case means world government.

The development of the social sciences and especially of a genuine social science of the international system, which is only in its infancy, is likely to have a substantial effect on the progress of the international system toward maturity. War is a crude, extremely expensive but often effective form of reality-testing, which has the added disadvantage of changing the reality to be tested. The improvement of the information system and the prevailing images of the international system that would follow from the development of a genuine social science of the international system would almost certainly have the effect of diminishing the probability of what might be called unintended war, that is, war that results from a lack of realism in the estimate of the consequences of decisions. Thus it is highly probable that the war of 1914 would not have occurred if the international system had possessed a more objective, carefully sampled, and adequately processed information system, which could have given the makers of a number of disastrous decisions a different image of the system. A more realistic image might have prevented these decisions, even without any change in ultimate values.

An improvement in the information system, however, would not leave ultimate values unchanged. The development, for instance, of a certain measure or index of success is likely to direct attention toward that aspect of the system which the index measures and to cause a high value to be placed on it. Thus the development of a way to measure the rate of economic growth has profoundly affected the valuation that many political decision-makers now place upon economic policy. Similarly, a measure of, shall we say, the general level of hostility in the international system, which would be quite within the present capability of the social sciences, might have a very profound effect not only on the image of the world held by the international decision-makers but also on the values they apply to it.

One word of hesitation and warning is worth making here, along the lines of Alexander Pope's admonition about a little learning. The image of the international system even in the best informed minds is subject to a large amount of uncertainty, and the decisions that are made in it should reflect the real uncertainties of the system. In a system of great uncertainty, he who hesitates is frequently saved. There is a danger that the techniques of the social sciences might be used to give an illusion of certainty where none exists. There is some evidence that war-gaming has had this effect, which could easily be disastrous. There is danger also that value systems are moved too easily in the direction of what is measurable and apparently known. Decision-making in systems as complex as the international system inevitably requires the operation of the unconscious as well as the conscious mind. The wisdom in decision-making that comes from wide experience and an almost unconscious appreciation of reality is not as good as explicit knowledge. Nevertheless when knowledge lingers, as it inevitably must, wisdom will have to do; and an attitude of mind that rejects wisdom in favor of imperfect knowledge may easily be disastrous. In this connection, the present tendency to try to develop rational modes of behavior in decision-making must be looked upon with a great deal of suspicion as well as some enthusiasm. Nevertheless, to reject knowledge where it exists in favor of a doubtful wisdom is no wisdom at all. The development of improved methods of collecting and processing information from the international system by such techniques as sample surveys, content analysis, correlation and factor analysis of complex systems, and the whole expansion of information processing and indexing that the computer makes possible is almost bound to have a maturing effect on the national images, both in regard to realism of content and humaneness of values.

The one possible cause for optimism about the international system is that there exists what might be called a "macro-learning" process, which seems to be cumulative in much the same way as science. It is only within the last 200 years, for instance, that we have achieved something that could be called a security community or stable peace in segments of the international system. During that period, we can trace something that looks like a progression from stable war into unstable war into unstable peace and finally into stable peace. As experience accumulates and as the memory of disastrous feedbacks affects present images of the system, these more mature images become a kind of folk wisdom that is transmitted from generation to generation, however precariously; and with the rise of genuinely scientific images of the international system we may expect this cumulative learning process to accelerate. It is reasonable to hope, therefore, that we may be fairly close to that key watershed in which the international system passes from a condition of unstable peace, albeit with enclaves of stable peace, into one in which stable peace becomes a property of the general system, which still however may have enclaves of unstable peace within it. At the moment, it must be admitted, the enclaves of stable peace appear as figures upon a ground of unstable peace. However, a little expansion of the figures to include, let us say, all of Europe, the United States, the Soviet Union, and Japan, and the ground will become the figure and the figure the ground. Quantitatively this change may be very small; yet it will be a watershed, and the system will never be the same again. One may then expect the enclaves of unstable peace to diminish as the learning process continues, until finally the vision of a world in stable peace, which has haunted mankind so elusively for so long, will finally be realized. When it is realized it will be the result of a long process of learning, in which cheap methods of learning such as science and perhaps even accumulated folk wisdom are substituted for the expensive methods of learning such as war.

OLE R. HOLSTI

Cognitive Dynamics and Images of the Enemy*

I

It is a basic theorem in the social sciences that "if men define situations as real, they are real in their consequences." Stated somewhat differently, the theorem asserts that an individual responds not only to the "objective" characteristics of a situation, but also to the meaning the situation has for him; the person's subsequent behavior and the results of that behavior are determined by the meaning ascribed to the situation.[1]

This theorem can be applied more specifically to the concept of the enemy. Enemies are those who are defined as such, and if one acts upon that interpretation, it is more than likely that the original definition will be confirmed: "It is an undeniable privilege of every man to prove himself in the right in the thesis that the world is his enemy; for if he reiterates it frequently enough and makes it the background of his conduct, he is bound eventually to be right."[2]

* This paper is drawn from sections of a full-scale study to be published in David J. Finlay, Ole R. Holsti, and Richard R. Fagen, *Enemies in Politics* (Chicago: Rand-McNally, 1967). Owing to space limitations, quantitative content-analysis data used to test a number of propositions have been omitted from this paper. The reader interested in the data and techniques used to obtain them should consult the book.

[1] Robert K. Merton, *Social Theory and Social Structure*, rev. ed. (New York: The Free Press of Glencoe, 1957), pp. 421-22.

[2] "X" (George F. Kennan), "The Sources of Soviet Conduct," *Foreign Affairs*, Vol. XXV (1947), p. 569.

Ole R. Holsti is assistant professor of political science and Associate Director of the Studies in International Conflict and Integration at Stanford University. He is a co-author of *Content Analysis: A Handbook with Applications for the Study of International Crisis* and of the forthcoming *Enemies in Politics*.

If the concept of the enemy is considered from the perspective of attitudes, one interesting problem is the manner in which attitudes about the
enemy are maintained or changed. The history of international relations
suggests two contradictory tendencies. On the one hand, just as there are
no permanent allies in international relations, there appear to be no
permanent enemies. During its history, the United States has fought wars
against Britain, France, Mexico, Spain, Germany, Italy, and Japan, all of
which are currently allies to some degree. Even the most enduring international antagonisms—for example, between France and Germany—have
eventually dissolved. Thus, it is clear that attitudes toward enemies do
change.

Although hostile relationships at the international level are not eternal,
it is also evident that they tend to endure well past the first conciliatory
gestures. This resistance to changes in attitudes may be attributed to a
number of factors, not the least of which is an apparently universal
tendency to judge the actions of others—and particularly of those defined
as enemies—according to different standards from those applied to oneself.
Because friends are expected to be friendly and enemies to be hostile, there
is a tendency to view their behavior in line with these expectations. When
the other party is viewed within the framework of an "inherent bad faith"[3]
model the image of the enemy is clearly self-perpetuating, for the model itself denies the existence of data that could disconfirm it. At the inter-
personal level such behavior is characterized as abnormal—paranoia.
Different standards seem to apply at the international level; inherent-bad-
faith models are not considered abnormal, and even their underlying
assumptions often escape serious questioning.

This paper reports a case study of the cognitive dynamics associated
with images of the enemy. The basic hypothesis—that there exist cognitive
processes that tend to sustain such images—will be examined through study
of a single individual, former Secretary of State John Foster Dulles, and
his attitude toward a single "enemy," the Soviet Union. One point should
be made explicit at the outset: there is no intent here to indicate that Secretary Dulles' attitudes or behavior were in any way "abnormal." It is

---

[3] This term, derived from Henry A. Kissinger, *The Necessity for Choice* (Garden
City: Doubleday & Co., 1962), p. 201, is used here to denote a conception of the other
nation by which it is defined as evil *whatever* the nature of its actions—"damned if it
does, and damned if it doesn't." The reverse model is that of appeasement; all actions
of the other party, regardless of their character, are interpreted as non-hostile. Despite
some notable examples of appeasement, such as the Munich settlement prior to World
War II, misinterpretation deriving from the appeasement model seems to be relatively
rare at the international level.

precisely because of the assumption that his attitudes and behavior were within the normal range of high-ranking policy-makers that he was selected for intensive study. Thus, though Dulles was a unique personality in many respects, this research was undertaken on the premise that the findings may have implications for foreign-policy decision-making in general.

Primary data for this study were derived from the verbatim transcripts of all publicly available statements made by Dulles during the years 1953-1959, including 122 press conferences, 70 addresses, 67 appearances at Congressional hearings, and 166 other documents. This documentation was supplemented by contemporary newspapers, secondary sources, questionnaires sent to a number of Dulles' closest associates, and memoirs written by those who worked closely with him.[4]

II

The theoretical framework for this study has been developed from two major sources. The first and more general of these is the literature on the relationship of an individual's "belief system" to perception and action. The belief system, composed of a number of "images" of the past, present, and future, includes "all the accumulated, organized knowledge that the organism has about itself and the world."[5] It may be thought of as the set of lenses through which information concerning the physical and social environment is received. It orients the individual to his environment, defining it for him and identifying for him its salient characteristics. National images may be considered as subparts of the belief system. Like the belief system itself, these are models that order for the observer what would otherwise be an unmanageable amount of information.

All images are stereotyped in the trivial sense that they oversimplify reality. It is this characteristic that makes images functional—and can render them dysfunctional. Unless the *content* of the image coincides in some way with what is commonly perceived as reality, decisions based on these images are not likely to fulfill the actor's expectations. Erroneous images may also prove to have a distorting effect by encouraging reinterpretation

[4] For example, Sherman Adams, *Firsthand Report* (New York: Harper, 1961); Emmet John Hughes, *The Ordeal of Power* (New York: Atheneum, 1963); and Andrew Berding, *Dulles on Diplomacy* (Princeton: Van Nostrand, 1965). Berding, Assistant Secretary of State for Public Affairs, took extensive shorthand notes that reveal a remarkable similarity between Dulles' public and private views. The Eisenhower and Nixon memoirs have also been consulted, but these are notably lacking in any insight into Dulles' personality or beliefs.

[5] George A. Miller, Eugene Galanter, and Karl H. Pribram, *Plans and the Structure of Behavior* (New York: Holt, 1960), p. 16. See also, Kenneth E. Boulding, *The Image* (Ann Arbor: University of Michigan Press, 1956).

of information that does not fit the image; this is most probable with such inherent-bad-faith models as "totalitarian communism" or "monopolistic capitalism," which exclude the very types of information that might lead to a modification or clarification of the models themselves. Equally important is the *structure* of the belief system, which, along with its component images, is in continual interaction with new information. In general, the impact of this information depends upon the degree to which the structure of the belief system is "open" or "closed."[6]

Further insight and more specific propositions concerning the relationship between the belief system and new information can be derived from the theoretical and experimental literature on the cognitive dynamics associated with attitude change, and more specifically, from those theories that have been described as "homeostatic" or "balance theories." Among the most prominent of these are theories that postulate a "tendency toward balance," a "stress toward symmetry," a "tendency toward increased congruity," and a "reduction of cognitive dissonance."[7] Despite terminological differences, common to all these theories is the premise that imbalance between various components of attitude is psychologically uncomfortable.

Attitudes, which can be defined as "predispositions to respond in a particular way toward a specified class of objects," consist of both cognitive (beliefs) and affective (feelings) components.[8] Beliefs and feelings are mutually interdependent. A person with strong positive or negative affect toward an object is also likely to maintain a cognitive structure consistent with that affect. The reverse relationship is also true. Thus new information that challenges the pre-existing balance between feelings and beliefs generates intrapersonal tension and a concomitant pressure to restore an internally consistent belief system by reducing the discrepancy in some manner, *but not necessarily through a change in attitude.*

A stable attitude about the enemy is one in which feelings and beliefs are congruent and reinforce each other. An interesting problem results

[6] Milton Rokeach, *The Open and Closed Mind* (New York: Basic Books, 1960), p. 50.
[7] Fritz Heider, "Attributes and Cognitive Organization," *Journal of Psychology,* Vol. XXI (1946), pp. 107-12; Theodore M. Newcomb, "An Approach to the Study of Communicative Acts," *Psychological Review,* Vol. LX (1953), pp. 393-404; Charles E. Osgood and Percy H. Tannenbaum, "The Principle of Congruity in the Prediction of Attitude Change," *Psychological Review,* Vol. LXII (1955), pp. 42-55; Leon Festinger, *A Theory of Cognitive Dissonance* (Evanston, Ill.: Row, Peterson, 1957).
[8] Milton J. Rosenberg, "Cognitive Structure and Attitudinal Affect," *Journal of Abnormal and Social Psychology,* Vol. LIII (1956), pp. 367-72; and Milton J. Rosenberg, "A Structural Theory of Attitude Change," *Public Opinion Quarterly,* Vol. XXIV (1960), pp. 319-40. The definition of attitude used here is derived from Rosenberg, Carl I. Hovland, William J. McGuire, Robert P. Abelson, and Jack W. Brehm, *Attitude Organization and Change* (New Haven: Yale University Press, 1960), p. 1.

when information incongruent with pre-existing attitudes is received. What happens, for example, when the other party is perceived to be acting in a conciliatory manner, a cognition that is inconsistent with the definition of the enemy as evil? According to the various balance theories, a number of strategies may be used to reduce this discrepancy between affect and cognition. The source of discrepant information may be *discredited*, thereby denying its truth or relevance. However, denial may be difficult if it involves too great a distortion of reality; denial is perhaps most likely to occur when the discrepant information is ambiguous, or when its source is not considered credible. Receipt of information not consistent with one's attitudes may lead to a *search for other information* that supports the pre-existing balance. The challenge to pre-existing attitudes about an object may lead a person to *stop thinking* about it, or at least to reduce its salience to a point where it is no longer uncomfortable to live with the incongruity. This strategy seems most likely if the attitude object has low ego-relevance for the person. It has been pointed out, for example, that the remoteness of international relations for most individuals places them under very little pressure to resolve incongruities in their attitudes.[9] The person whose beliefs are challenged by new information may engage in *wishful thinking* by changing his beliefs to accord with his desires. The new information may be *reinterpreted* in a manner that will conform with and substantiate pre-existing attitudes rather than contradict them. The process of reinterpreting new and favorable information about a disliked person is illustrated in the following dialogue:

> Mr. X: The trouble with Jews is that they only take care of their own group.
>
> Mr. Y: But the records of the Community Chest show that they give more generously than non-Jews.
>
> Mr. X: That shows that they are always trying to buy favor and intrude in Christian affairs. They think of nothing but money; that is why there are so many Jewish bankers.
>
> Mr. Y: But a recent study shows that the per cent of Jews in banking is proportionally much smaller than the per cent of non-Jews.
>
> Mr. X: That's just it. They don't go in for respectable business. They would rather run night clubs.[10]

[9] William A. Scott, "Rationality and Non-rationality of International Attitudes," *Journal of Conflict Resolution*, Vol. II (1958), pp. 8-16.

[10] Gordon W. Allport, *The Nature of Prejudice*, quoted in Robert B. Zajonc, "The Concepts of Balance, Congruity, and Dissonance," *Public Opinion Quarterly*, Vol. XXIV (1960), p. 281.

Discrepant information may also be *differentiated* into two or more sub-categories, with a strong dissociative relationship between them. Whereas strategies such as discrediting discrepant information appear to be most germane for situations of limited and ambiguous information, differentiation is likely to occur in the opposite situation. Abundant information "equips the individual to make minor (and hair-splitting) adjustments which minimize the degree of change in generalized affect toward the object. . . . Upon receipt of new information, a person is more agile in producing 'yes, but . . .' responses when he is well informed about an object than when he is poorly informed."[11]

Finally, the new and incongruent information may be accepted, leading one to *modify or change his pre-existing attitudes* so as to establish a new, balanced attitude-structure.

One difficulty with balance theories as described to this point is that any and all data—attitude change or resistance to attitude change through a variety of strategies—appear to support them. If the theories are to be meaningful, they should enable the investigator to predict which of the outcomes discussed above is likely to take place under specified circumstances. At least four factors related to persuasibility have been identified: the *content* and *source* of the discrepant information, the *situation*, and the *personality* of the recipient.[12] A further discussion of these four factors in conjunction with their relevance to John Foster Dulles will permit the development of specific propositions about his attitudes toward the Soviet Union and the effects of new information on these attitudes.

Content factors. All discrepant information does not create an equal pressure to reduce dissonance. Attitudes about central values will be more resistant to change because of the introduction of discrepant information than those at the periphery of the belief system. Tolerance for incongruity is lowest and, therefore, the pressure for dissonance reduction is highest if the attitude object is highly salient for goal attainment. Attitudes that support important values, such as self-acceptance, tend to remain unchanged even in a high dissonance situation. Thus predictions concerning the effects of incongruent information about an attitude object presuppose some knowledge of the person's belief system and the relationship of the attitude object to central values in the belief system.

In his memoirs, Anthony Eden describes Dulles as "a preacher in a world

---

[11] Theodore M. Newcomb, quoted in Richard E. Walton and Robert B. McKersie, *Attitude Change and Intergroup Relations,* Herman C. Krannert Graduate School of Industrial Administration, Purdue University, Institute Paper No. 86, Oct. 1964, p. 53.

[12] Rosenberg *et al., op. cit.,* pp. 215-21.

of politics."[13] Of the many attributes in Dulles' belief system it is perhaps this "theological" world view that was most germane to his conception of the enemy. It is clear that the Soviet Union represented the antithesis of the values that were at the core of his belief system. An associate recalled that "the Secretary's profound and fervent opposition to the doctrine and ambitions of communism was heightened by the fact that communism was atheistic."[14] The distinction between moral and political bases for evaluating the Soviet Union was blurred, if not totally obliterated. The more Dulles' image of the Soviet Union was dominated by moral rather than political criteria, the more likely it would be that new information at odds with this model would be reinterpreted to conform with the image, leaving his basic views intact.

Situational factors. An individual may hold inconsistent attitudes without discomfort if he is not compelled to attend to the discrepancy. But he may find himself in a situation that continually forces him to examine both information at odds with his attitudes and any inconsistency arising therefrom.

That Dulles' position as Secretary of State constantly forced him to examine every aspect of Soviet foreign policy is a point requiring no further elaboration. As a result, any discrepancies in his attitudes toward the Soviet Union were continually brought to his attention, presumably creating some pressure to reduce the dissonance created by incongruent information. Persons who are required to express their attitudes in public may be under greater constraint to maintain or restore a balance between components of attitudes; this pressure may be heightened if the situation is one in which a high social value is placed on consistency.[15] Again it is clear that the office of Secretary of State required frequent public interpretations of Soviet policy. These statements were in turn scrutinized and evaluated for consistency by the press, Congress, interested publics, and allies. Thus situational factors would have made it difficult for Dulles to withdraw his attention from any discrepancies in those attitudes.

Source factors. Responses to new information are related to the perceived credibility of the communicator; the higher the credibility of the source and the more he is esteemed, the more likely is the audience to be persuaded.[16]

[13] Anthony Eden, *Full Circle* (Boston: Houghton-Mifflin, 1960), p. 71.

[14] Berding, *op. cit.*, p. 162. See also, Hughes, *op. cit.*, 204-06.

[15] Rosenberg *et al.*, *op. cit.*, pp. 220-21.

[16] Carl I. Hovland, Irving L. Janis, and Harold H. Kelley, *Communication and Persuasion* (New Haven: Yale University Press, 1953), pp. 19-55.

Dulles considered Soviet communicators to be generally unreliable, an opinion sustained both by the record of Soviet propaganda and by his judgment that "atheists can hardly be expected to conform to an ideal so high"[17] as truth. The fact that much of the information which might be at odds with Dulles' image of the U.S.S.R. originated with the Soviets themselves tended to diminish rather than enhance the probability of attitude change; unless the truth of the information was beyond question, it was likely to be discredited owing to its source.

Personality factors. Persuasibility exists as a factor independent of content.[18] That is, certain personality types can be more easily persuaded than others to change their attitudes. Individuals also appear to differ in their tolerance for dissonance and tend to use different means to re-establish stable attitudes. There is also evidence that persons with low self-esteem and general passivity are more easily persuaded to alter their attitudes. With such persons, "a previously stabilized attitude will be maintained at low levels of certainty and confidence. Such persons will also be more likely to 'submit' to others who claim for themselves some status as authority or expert."[19] On the other hand, persons with high self-esteem are inclined to decrease their search for information under stress.[20]

Data on attributes of Dulles' personality that might be relevant to the problem of attitude change are necessarily fragmentary and anecdotal rather than systematic. The problem is perhaps compounded by the controversy that surrounded him. Both critics and admirers seem to agree, however, that Dulles placed almost absolute reliance on his own abilities to conduct American foreign policy. He felt, with considerable justification, that his family background and his own career had provided him with exceptional training for the position of Secretary of State. Intensive study of the Marxist-Leninist classics added to his belief that he was uniquely qualified to assess the meaning of Soviet policy. This sense of indispensability carried over into the day-to-day operations of policy formulation, and during his tenure as Secretary of State he showed a marked lack of receptivity to advice. One of his associates wrote:

> He was a man of supreme confidence within himself. . . . He simply
> did not pay any attention to staff or to experts or anything else. Maybe

[17] John Foster Dulles, *War or Peace* (New York: Macmillan, 1950), p. 20.
[18] Irving L. Janis *et al., Personality and Persuasibility* (New Haven: Yale University Press, 1959).
[19] Ivan D. Steiner and Evan D. Rogers, "Alternative Responses to Dissonance," *Journal of Abnormal and Social Psychology*, Vol. LXVI (1963), pp. 128-36.
[20] Margaret G. Hermann, *Stress, Self-Esteem, and Defensiveness in an Internation Simulation* (China Lake, California: Project Michelson, 1965), p. 77.

in a very subconscious way he did catalog some of the information given him but he did not, as was characteristic of Acheson and several others of the Secretaries of State with whom I have worked, take the very best he could get out of his staff. . . .[21]

Using this summary of content, situational, source, and personality factors as a base, a number of specific predictions about Dulles' attitudes toward the Soviet Union can be derived. It seems clear that Dulles' role was one that placed a high premium on consistency between elements of his attitudes toward the Soviet Union. At the same time, despite information that might challenge his beliefs, any fundamental change in attitude would appear unlikely. As long as the Soviet Union remained a closed society ruled by Communists, it represented the antithesis of values at the core of Dulles' belief system. Furthermore, information that might challenge the inherent-bad-faith model of the Soviet Union generally came from the Soviets themselves—a low-credibility source—and was often ambiguous enough to accommodate more than one interpretation. Finally, the sparse evidence available is at least consistent with the theory that Dulles had a low-persuasibility personality.

Thus, on the basis of the theoretical framework developed earlier, three strategies for restoring a balance between his belief system and discrepant information appear most likely to have been used by Dulles: discrediting the source of the new information so as to be consistent with the belief system; searching for other information consistent with pre-existing attitudes; and differentiating between various elements in the Soviet Union.[22]

III

Dulles' views concerning the sources of Soviet foreign policy provide an almost classic example of differentiating the concept of the enemy into its good and bad components to maintain cognitive balance. His numerous statements indicate that he considered Soviet policy within a framework of three conflicting pairs of concepts: ideology vs. national interest; party vs. state; and rulers vs. people.

After Dulles had been temporarily retired to private life by his defeat in the New York senatorial election in 1949, he undertook his most extensive analysis of Soviet foreign policy in his book *War or Peace*. The source of that policy, he stated repeatedly, was to be found in the Stalinist and Len-

[21] Letter to author, Aug. 25, 1961.
[22] Only some of these techniques are illustrated in this paper. For further evidence, see Finlay, Holsti, and Fagen, *op. cit.*, Chap. 2.

inist exegeses of Marx's works. In particular, he cited Stalin's *Problems of Leninism*, which he equated with Hitler's *Mein Kampf* as a master plan of goals, strategy, and tactics, as the best contemporary guide to Soviet foreign policy. From a careful reading of that book, he concluded, one could understand both the character of Soviet leaders and the blueprint of Soviet policy. Characteristically, he placed special emphasis on the materialistic and atheistic aspects of the Communist creed, attributes that he felt ensured the absolute ruthlessness of Soviet leaders in their quest for world domination. By the time Dulles took office as Secretary of State in 1953 he had clearly adopted the theory that Soviet policy was the manifestation of ideology. His six years in office appear to have confirmed for him the validity of that view; it changed only in that it became stronger with the passing of time.

The second dichotomy in Dulles' thinking concerning the sources of Soviet foreign policy—the Russian state vs. the Communist Party—paralleled the concepts of national interest and Marxist ideology. He often pointed to the existence of a conflict of interests and, therefore, of policies between party and state. It was to the Communist Party rather than to the Russian state that he attributed Soviet aggressiveness, asserting that the state was simply the tool of the party. During his testimony at the hearings in early 1957 on the Eisenhower Doctrine for the Middle East, the following dialogue took place.

> Secretary Dulles: I say countries controlled by international communism.
>
> Senator Jackson: Yes. Well, they are synonymous [with 'Soviet'] but for the purpose—
>
> Secretary Dulles: No, it is much broader. . . . international communism is a conspiracy composed of a certain number of people, all of whose names I do not know, and many of whom I suppose are secret. They have gotten control of one government after another. They first got control of Russia after the first World War. They have gone on getting control of one country after another until finally they were stopped. But they have not gone out of existence. . . .
>
> Senator Jackson: Would you not agree on this: that international communism has been used as an instrument of Russian foreign policy since 1918?
>
> Secretary Dulles: I would put it the other way around. Russian foreign policy is an instrument of international communism.[23]

[23] Senate Committees on Foreign Relations and Armed Services, *Hearings* (Jan. 15, 1957), pp. 176-77.

Cognitive Dynamics and Images of the Enemy

From the distinction between party and state Dulles deduced that Soviet hostility toward the United States existed only on the top level of the party hierarchy and that, but for the party, friendly relations between Russia and the United States could be achieved.

The third dichotomy in Dulles' theory of Soviet foreign policy was that of the Russian people vs. the Soviet leaders. As in the case of the distinction between party and state, in which he equated the former with hostility toward the United States, he believed that the enmity of the Soviet leadership was in no way shared by the Russian people. At no time did he suggest anything but the highest degree of friendship between the Russian people and the free world. Typical of his view was the statement that: "There is no dispute at all between the United States and the peoples of Russia. If only the Government of Russia was interested in looking out for the welfare of Russia, the people of Russia, we would have a state of non-tension right away."[24] By asserting that the rulers of the Soviet Union, as Communists, enjoyed little public support, Dulles laid the groundwork for the further assumption that, were Soviet leaders responsive to Russian public opinion, Soviet-American differences would be negligible.[25]

This theory, however, directly contradicted another of his propositions concerning Soviet foreign policy. Discussing Khrushchev's sensational revelations about the Stalin era in 1956, he commented that a Stalinist dictatorship was tolerated as long as it was gaining external triumphs, as was true from 1945 to 1950.[26] That interpretation, made in the course of a declaration that Soviet policy had gone bankrupt in the face of free-world firmness, is not wholly compatible with a theory of absolute divergence of interests between people and rulers.

Dulles' views regarding the sources of Soviet foreign policy lend support to the proposition that a stable attitude-structure can be maintained by

[24] John Foster Dulles, "Interview in Great Britain," *State Department Bulletin* (hereafter cited as *SDB*), Vol. XXXIX (Nov. 10, 1958), p. 734.

[25] This is precisely the position that the Soviet leaders have taken toward the nations of the free world. For example, after the U-2 incident Khrushchev stated: "Even now I profoundly believe that the American people, with the exception of certain imperialists and monopolist circles, want peace and desire friendship with the Soviet Union. . . . I do not doubt President Eisenhower's earnest desire for peace. But although the President is endowed with supreme executive power in the U.S.A., there are evidently circles that are circumscribing him." Nikita Khrushchev, "May 5 Report," *The Current Digest of the Soviet Press*, Vol. XII, No. 18 (June 1, 1960), pp. 17, 19. A detailed review of Soviet images of the United States may be found in Ralph K. White, "Images in the Context of International Conflict: Soviet Perceptions of the U.S. and the U.S.S.R.," *International Behavior*, ed. by Herbert C. Kelman (New York: Holt, Rinehart & Winston, 1965), pp. 236-76.

[26] John Foster Dulles, "News Conference of June 27, 1956," *SDB*, Vol. XXXV (July 9, 1956), p. 48.

differentiating the concept of the enemy. Moreover, it was consistent with Dulles' proclivity for viewing the world in moral terms that the various characteristics of the Soviet Union were differentiated into the categories of good and evil. The former, which in his view played little part in actual Soviet policy-formulation, consisted of the policy of the Russian state, grounded in a concern for Russia's national interest and representing the aspirations of the Russian people. Rarely, if ever, did he represent these as being hostile toward the free world. The second set of interests that Dulles felt were represented in actual Soviet policy were Marxist ideology, the international conspiratorial party, and the Soviet rulers. These factors had completely dominated his thinking by the latter part of his term in office, and it was in them that he located the source of Soviet-American enmity.

A theory such as Dulles', which postulated a divergence of interests between party and state and between elites and masses, is pessimistic for short-term resolution of conflict. At the same time, the theory is optimistic for the long-term, for it suggests that competing national interests are virtually nonexistent. It assumes that, but for the intransigence of the Communist elite, Russia and the United States would coexist in harmony (Fig. 1). In this respect, his theory was in accord with what has been described as "the traditional American assumption that only a few evil leaders stood in the way of a worldwide acceptance of American values and hence of peace."[27]

IV

The proposition that information consistent with pre-existing attitudes is more readily accepted than that which is incongruent can be illustrated by

FIG. 1.

Dulles' Conception of Conflict Between
the Soviet Union and the Free World.

Parties to Conflict		Level of Conflict	Conflict Resolution
Free World	Soviet Union ruled by International Communists	Moral	No resolution possible
Free World	Russia ruled by national elites	Political	Resolved by traditional methods
Free World	Russian people	No conflict exists owing to moral consensus	

[27] Eric F. Goldman, *The Crucial Decade—And After* (New York: Vintage Books, 1960), p. 250.

Cognitive Dynamics and Images of the Enemy

a more detailed examination of Dulles' views concerning various elements of Soviet capabilities: military, technological, political, economic, popular support, and external support. Two further factors beyond Dulles' belief system must also be considered: How ambiguous was the information, and how easily could it be confirmed by data from sources other than the Soviet Union? Because Dulles considered the Soviets a low-credibility source, there should be a tendency to discount information on Soviet strength unless independent verification was available.

On the basis of Dulles' belief system it was predicted that information about those elements of Soviet strength that contribute to and sustain the inherent-bad-faith model and that can be verified would be accepted most readily. Technological and military elements of strength meet both requirements; such capabilities are compatible with the image of a hostile and threatening enemy, and are relatively easily verified by independent data. On the other hand, those attributes of the Soviet system about which information is most ambiguous, or which tend to lend "legitimacy" to the regime, would be perceived as weak. Such factors as morale, loyalty, prestige, and goodwill—all of which are implied in the categories of "internal support" and "external support"—are difficult to evaluate, in part owing to the paucity of independent sources of data. Moreover, a high assessment of Soviet strength on these factors would be at odds with that aspect of Dulles' image of the Soviet Union which predicted an absolute divergence between the Russian people and their Communist rulers. In summary, then, the hypothesis predicts an evaluation of Soviet capabilities that would be most compatible with the image of a garrison state with ample capabilities for aggression, but internally weak owing to the absence of economic strength, political stability, and support for the regime from within or without. A more precise explication of the hypothesis is presented in Fig. 2.

FIG. 2.

Hypothesized Assessment of Soviet Capabilities

Element of Soviet Power	Congruity with "Inherent Bad Faith" Model	Ambiguity of Information	Sources of Independent Data	Hypothesized Assessment By Dulles
Military	High	Low	Many	Strong
Technology	High	Low	Many	Strong
Economy	Intermediate	Intermediate	Intermediate	Intermediate
Political	Intermediate	Intermediate	Intermediate	Intermediate
Popular Support	Low	High	Few	Weak
External Support	Low	High	Few	Weak

Dulles' evaluation of Soviet armed forces and military strength was consistently high. Without disregarding Soviet capabilities in atomic weapons, he repeatedly pointed to the huge land forces at the disposal of the Kremlin as the major threat to the West, a threat heightened by the mobility of these forces within the perimeter of the Sino-Soviet world. He felt that neither in size nor in mobility could the more dispersed armies of the West match those of the Soviet Union and its satellites. This assessment was in large part the underlying rationale for the Dulles doctrine of "massive retaliation," which was designed to neutralize the preponderant Communist strength for conventional and guerrilla types of warfare.

If Dulles had any doubts about the military strength of the Soviet Union they were, as might be expected, with respect to its loyalty. In 1952 he stated that the "Communist leaders of Russia are almost as afraid of the Red Army as we are."[28] These doubts notwithstanding, Dulles' statements on the Soviet military are notably lacking in the ringing pronouncements of impotence that often characterized his assessment of other elements of Soviet power.

Dulles generally had a high regard for Soviet technology, particularly for that sector with implications for military strength. As with many Americans, any doubts about Soviet capabilities disappeared after the successful launching of Sputnik I in the autumn of 1957. In 1953 he had expressed some skepticism about the first Soviet claim to having exploded a hydrogen bomb, but four years later, when questioned about the veracity of the announced claim of a successfully tested intercontinental ballistic missile, he replied, "I would assume that there are facts which underlie this statement. *In general the Soviet statements in this area have had some supporting facts.*"[29]

During the middle years of his term in office, Dulles perceived Soviet strength as deteriorating markedly, a decline attributed largely to economic weakness. He insisted that the Soviet Union was staggering under an impossible economic burden that had forced its leadership to seek a respite in the cold war. It was in this area that Dulles located the major cause of the impending "collapse" of the Soviet regime; one of his associates recalled that Dulles "felt it [the Soviet system] would eventually break on the

---

[28] *Congressional Record*, 82nd Cong., 2nd Sess., p. 1801.
[29] John Foster Dulles, "News Conference, Aug. 12, 1953," *SDB*, Vol. XXIX (Aug. 24, 1953), p. 236 (italics added); and Dulles, "News Conference, Aug. 27, 1957," *SDB*, Vol. XXXVII (Sept. 16, 1957), p. 458.

Cognitive Dynamics and Images of the Enemy

rigidities of its economic system."[30] This belief was clearly revealed in his Congressional testimony just before the Geneva summit meeting of 1955.

> They [the Soviets] have been constantly hoping and expecting our economy was going to collapse in some way, due to what they regard as the inherent defects in the capitalistic system, or due to over-expenditure, and the like. *On the contrary, it has been their system that is on the point of collapsing.*[31]

Hence he was initially quite optimistic concerning the Soviet shift toward the use of economic tactics in foreign policy. His first reaction was that Soviet offers of aid to underdeveloped areas were a bluff to force the United States into bidding against the Soviet Union and, in the end, into spending itself into bankruptcy. He characterized that economic offensive as an admission of weakness rather than a sign of strength, stating that the Soviet Union had neither the intention nor the ability to carry out all of its foreign-aid commitments. At the December 1955 meeting of the NATO Council, Dulles predicted that the free world would defeat Soviet economic moves in the Middle East because the Soviet Union had a deficit in its balance of trade. Under these circumstances it was agreed to offer Colonel Gamal Abdul Nasser of Egypt a loan—eighty per cent to be financed by the United States—for building a dam at Aswan, in order to reap some of the propaganda advantages that had accrued to the Soviet Union through far less grandiose projects.

The Egyptian government, however, contracted for the purchase of Soviet-bloc arms, recognized the Peoples' Republic of China, and made unfriendly gestures toward both Israel and the Suez Canal. Although Dulles had been tolerant of Egyptian diplomacy only weeks earlier, stating that Nasser was "actuated primarily by a desire to maintain the genuine independence of the area,"[32] Nasser's increasing reliance upon Soviet aid was not so easily forgiven.

With the tacit support of a Congress increasingly uncomfortable about the prospects of competition from higher Egyptian cotton production and the precarious survival of Israel, he decided upon Egypt as the place to call the bluff of Soviet economic aid. C. D. Jackson, a presidential foreign-policy adviser, revealed that the Aswan offer was cancelled to provoke a showdown with the Soviet Union.[33] Thus, partly on the basis of his evalu-

[30] Letter to author, Aug. 25, 1961.
[31] House Subcommittee of the Committee on Appropriations, *Hearings* (June 10, 1955), p. 10. Emphasis added.
[32] John Foster Dulles, "News Conference, Apr. 3, 1956," *SDB*, Vol. XXXIV (Apr. 16, 1956), p. 640.
[33] *Toronto Globe Mail*, Mar. 13, 1957, 1:2-5.

ation of Soviet economic weakness, he abruptly cancelled the Aswan Dam offer, setting off a chain of events that was to culminate in the tripartite invasion of Egypt.

In many respects, Dulles' conduct during the Middle East crisis was most revealing of certain facets of his personality and belief system. It was based upon an almost unshakeable conviction that the Soviet Union was economically weak and upon a belief in the efficacy of "brinkmanship" to defeat Soviet policy. It was a period during which he relied largely upon his own instincts rather than upon the advice of others. Henry A. Byroade, American Ambassador to Egypt, was never consulted, perhaps because he had made known his opposition to the cancellation of the Aswan offer. In fact, Byroade did not know of the decision until he read of it in Cairo newspapers. Byroade called the Aswan Dam "a feasible project" that would be beneficial to our relations with Egypt and the Middle East, the cancellation of which was "a mistake."[34] The French Ambassador's attempts to warn Dulles of the probable consequences of his decision, two days prior to the cancellation, were greeted by Dulles with derision. The announcement of cancellation was made in such a manner as to maximize the humiliation of Colonel Nasser by casting doubts on the ability of the Egyptian economy to absorb the American aid. And finally, after the tragic episode had run full cycle, Dulles was prepared—as he had not been after his earlier "triumphs at the brink"—to give full credit to the Senate Appropriations Committee, which he claimed had forced him to cancel the Aswan offer.[35]

As much as a year after the Suez episode, Dulles was still adamantly insisting that the Soviet economy was weak because of serious imbalances. He was especially inclined to suggest that the effort to gain rocket and missile parity with the United States had placed an intolerable burden upon the economy, a contention for which, however, he relied upon such evidence as the low Russian automobile production figures. Thus, it was largely in the realm of economics that he located the "fatal weakness" in the Soviet regime.

Only during his final year in office was Dulles' estimate of Soviet economic strength revised upward. The continuing Russian economic offensive, which proved to be more than mere bluff, the increased evidence of a rising Russian standard of living, coupled with Premier Khrushchev's contention that he would "bury" the free world under the products of his economy, appear to have had a marked effect upon his attitude. By mid-

[34] Senate Committees on Foreign Relations and Armed Services, *Hearings* (Feb. 7, 1957), pp. 708, 714, 717, and 752.
[35] Senate Appropriations Committee, *Hearings* (Aug. 19, 1957), pp. 610-11.

Cognitive Dynamics and Images of the Enemy

1958, he referred to a Russian "economic breakthrough" and to the Soviet intention to become the world's greatest producer of consumer goods.

Why did Dulles' evaluation of the Soviet economy change so dramatically in 1958, while other aspects of his attitude remained constant? In terms of the typology presented in Fig. 2, the evidence beyond mere Soviet claims was so overwhelming that denial of its validity was no longer possible. Even Dulles must have recognized that his predictions of economic collapse, made only three years earlier, were no longer tenable.

Dulles' evaluation of Soviet political and diplomatic strength was an ambivalent one, in which he perceived both institutional strengths and weaknesses as well as varying capabilities among individual leaders. He felt that Soviet goals were institutionalized in the Communist Party and in the works of Marx, Lenin, and Stalin, and not, like those of the Nazis, dependent upon the idiosyncracies of one unstable man. Following the death of Stalin, however, his estimate changed in that his attention was focused more on the intra-Kremlin cliques and the "despotic disarray" among Stalin's heirs. Dulles' reaction to such events was a curious mixture of hope and fear. On the one hand, he welcomed maneuverings for personal power within the Kremlin on two grounds: they tended to confirm his theory of weakness and instability within the Soviet Union, and he interpreted much of the infighting as a challenge by those who represented the forces of enlightenment within the Soviet Union (national interest and more consumer goods) against the forces of evil (international Communism and continued emphasis on heavy industry). On the other hand, he appeared to fear the consequences of de-Stalinization on the Western Alliance. When Beria was arrested in mid-1953, Dulles told the Cabinet: "This is the kind of time when we ought to be *doubling* our bets, not reducing them—as all the western parliaments want to do. This is the time to *crowd* the enemy—and maybe *finish* him, once and for all. But if we're dilatory, he can consolidate—and probably put us right back where we were."[36]

Dulles' most unequivocal assessment of Soviet weakness was in the area of popular and external support. Not one of his recorded statements indicates that he believed there was any support whatever by the masses of the Russian people for the Soviet regime. This was completely consistent with his prior assumption that there was no conflict of interest between the Russian people, who were basically friendly to the free world, and the United States. The corollary to this premise was that Soviet hostility and

[36] Cabinet meeting of July 10, 1953, quoted in Hughes, *op. cit.*, p. 137. Emphasis in the source.

aggressiveness derived only from the designs of a small clique of leaders. Thus, the Russian people were assumed to be not only dissatisfied with domestic conditions but also opposed to the Soviet orientation in foreign policy.

Dulles had mixed feelings about the increment added to Soviet power by other Communist nations. His most serious criticism of the Truman Administration during the 1952 campaign had been against the "sterile" policy of containment, which did not envision an offensive to liberate the captives of international Communism. The proclaimed policy was based upon the premise that moral support from the free world would enable patriots within the Communist world to bring "nationalist" regimes to power. Despite his sometimes intemperate language—he was reprimanded by General Eisenhower during the campaign for his failure to qualify his discussion of liberation with the word "peaceful" in one of his speeches[37]— it is highly unlikely that he ever intended the "rollback" to be accomplished by the force of arms.

The meaning of liberation received its first test in June 1953 when riots in East Germany threatened to destroy Soviet control of that satellite state. By October 1956, just prior to the Hungarian Revolution, Dulles spoke as one who, trapped by his own campaign slogan, had come to realize the truth in the London *Economist's* assertion that, "Unhappily, 'liberation' entails no risk of war only when it means nothing." On October 21, 1956, when questioned about events in Eastern Europe, Dulles devoted a great deal of time to emphasizing that the Soviet Union could *legally* as well as practically move troops into the area and that there was little the United States was prepared to do in any eventuality. Six days later he made a special point of stressing peaceful American intentions in Eastern Europe. He refused, however, to consider any bargain that would involve Soviet withdrawal of troops from the area in exchange for some American concessions.[38] The events of November 1956 removed all doubts about the meaning of liberation, confirming what had become obvious in 1953 when the East German rioting was met with offers of Red Cross food packages to the Ulbricht government.

Thus Dulles' evaluation of Soviet capabilities was consistent with his thinking on other aspects of the Soviet Union. His assessment of Soviet

[37] Hughes, *op. cit.*, pp. 70-71; and Adams, *op. cit.*, p. 88.
[38] Hans J. Morgenthau, in *An Uncertain Tradition*, ed. by Norman A. Graebner (New York: McGraw-Hill, 1961), p. 293; John Foster Dulles, "Face the Nation," (Oct. 21, 1956), mimeo., pp. 1-7; Dulles, "The Task of Waging Peace," *SDB*, Vol. XXXV (Nov. 5, 1956), pp. 698-99; and G. Barraclough, "More than Dulles Must Go," *Nation*, Vol. CLXXXVI (Jan. 25, 1958), p. 69.

military and technological capabilities was consistently high, and there is evidence that he interpreted new information, such as the breakthrough in Soviet rocketry, with a realism not always shared by his colleagues. As was suggested in the hypothesis, new information in the military area of Soviet power was least ambiguous and most easily verified by external sources. At the same time, such information was not inconsistent with his pre-existing attitude toward the Soviet Union.

On the other hand, certain other elements of Soviet capabilities were consistently rated as weak. Dulles' overall evaluation of Soviet strength may have been valid in many respects. However, there is some question whether his views on the Soviet economy or popular support were totally realistic, even admitting the unevenness of Soviet economic development and the certainty of some dissatisfaction with Soviet dictatorship—be it of the harsh Stalinist type or of the more relaxed Khrushchevian model. In both cases, he appeared far more prone to accept information tending to confirm his beliefs of economic impotence and popular resistance than information to the contrary. He readily accepted, for example, almost any hint of agricultural trouble within the Soviet Union, but it was a long time before he regarded Soviet foreign aid as anything but a sign of weakness and failure. Not until long after the disaster of Suez did he reassess his earlier evaluation; only then did he conclude that the Soviet economy had achieved a "breakthrough." Whereas his attitude regarding the Soviet economy had changed by 1958, he never rejected his long-standing theory that the Soviet regime was wholly without support from the Russian people.

V

These findings concerning Dulles' views on the Soviet Union are generally consistent with research on attitude change carried out within the framework of "cognitive balance" theories under rigorous experimental conditions. But the relevance of either the theory or the findings for international politics is somewhat less evident.

At the beginning of this paper it was asserted that "enemies are those whom we define as such." This is not to say, however, that images of the enemy are necessarily unrealistic or that they can be attributed solely to an individual's belief system.[39] Soviet policy itself was clearly an important source of Dulles' images, and his definition of the Soviet Union as an enemy was in many respects a realistic one. During his tenure of office, from 1953

[39] Except, of course, in abnormal cases such as paranoia. These are, however, outside the scope of this paper.

to 1959, the Soviet Union did represent a potential threat to the United States; the cold war was not merely a product of Dulles' imagination, nor can the development of Soviet-American relations during the period be explained solely by reference to his belief system.[40]

Another question also arises: To what extent do policy decisions reflect attributes of those who made them? The assertion that personal characteristics are crucial to politics because political decisions are made by individuals is as trivial as it is true. If it were demonstrated that other factors (role, organization, culture, and the like) account for an overwhelming proportion of the variance in the formulation of foreign-policy decisions, then findings about individual behavior would be peripheral to international politics.

Although a decision-maker carries with him into office a complex of personal values, beliefs, and attitudes, even a high-ranking official such as the Secretary of State is subject to bureaucratic constraints. These range from constitutional and legal requirements to informal, but nevertheless real, limitations rooted in the expectations of his associates. The organizational context may influence the premises and information upon which the incumbent makes his decisions in a number of ways: organizational goals tend to endure beyond the tenure of a single individual; pressures for policy continuity can affect the interpretation of new information; colleagues and subordinates can serve as important sources of values and information; and the tendency of groups to impose conformity on its members is well documented. These constraints establish boundaries that restrict to a greater or lesser degree the scope of the incumbent's decisions and the criteria used to make them.

How much latitude is there, then, within which a single official's values and attitudes may significantly affect foreign-policy decisions?[41] In part

[40] More generally, a socio-psychological approach would provide an all-encompassing theory of international politics only if the prior assumption was made that all conflict results from distorted images of nations. Such a premise—in effect denying the existence of contradictory and mutually exclusive interests—is clearly untenable. For further elaboration of this point, see Herbert C. Kelman, "Social-Psychological Approaches to the Study of International Relations: The Question of Relevance," in Kelman (ed.), *op. cit.*, pp. 565-607.

[41] The assumption that the individual decision-maker has no freedom of action is often one aspect of the stereotyped images that Russians and Americans have of each other. According to the orthodox Marxist view of American politics, political figures of both parties are interchangeable, for they all represent the narrow interests of the capitalist ruling class. Similarly, Americans often tend to assume that all Soviet leaders are interchangeable cogs in a monolithic party-state structure. Dulles himself seemed to alternate between this view of the Soviet political process and the theory that the Kremlin was split between factions representing the "friendly Russian nationalists" and "hostile Communists."

this may depend on the nature of the situation and the ambiguity of relevant information. Decisions requiring only the application of well-established procedures are likely to reflect institutional routines rather than personal values. On the other hand, during an unanticipated situation in which decision time is short and information is ambiguous, the attitudes of a small group or even a single official will take on added significance.

The manner in which each decision-maker interprets his sphere of competence and perceives constraints upon it is also important. If he defines his role in narrow terms—for example, if he perceives his primary responsibility to be that of administering the Department of State rather than the formulation of policy—his influence on many issues will be concomitantly decreased. On the other hand, by defining his sphere of competence in broad terms, the decision-maker can increase his authority.

Dulles' admirers and critics agree that his impact on American foreign policy was second to none. Richard Rovere's judgment that "Mr. Dulles has exercised powers over American foreign policy similar to those exercised by Franklin D. Roosevelt during the war"[42] is supported by most students of the Eisenhower Administration. His brilliant mind and forceful personality, combined with an almost total reliance upon his own abilities and the strong support of the President, served to magnify his influence.

Dulles was keenly aware of the power structure in which he operated and was a zealous guardian of his position within it. He was most careful to ensure that no competing centers of influence were established. All four of President Eisenhower's White House aids on foreign policy—C. D. Jackson, Nelson A. Rockefeller, William Jackson, and Harold Stassen—left the government after clashing with Dulles, who perceived that they might become a threat to his position; he "watched these specialists intently and, at the first sign of what he suspected to be a possible threat to the tight and straight line-of-command between himself and the President, he straightened out the difficulty."[43] Nor did he brook any competition within his own department. It was reported that Henry Cabot Lodge's direct access to the President, through his unprecedented invitation to attend Cabinet meetings, was a source of friction between Lodge and Dulles. Also indicative is Christian Herter's remark that as Undersecretary he had been "No. 2 man in a one-man show."[44]

[42] Richard Rovere, "Dulles," *The New Yorker*, Vol. XXXV (Apr. 25, 1959), p. 95.
[43] Adams, *op. cit.*, p. 91. See also *The New York Times*, Feb. 25, 1953, 9:1, and Feb. 2, 1958, 1:4, 56:3.
[44] Thomas C. Kennedy, "The Making of a Secretary of State: John Foster Dulles," M.A. thesis, Stanford University, 1959, p. 21.

Dulles' care in guarding the prerogatives of his office was neither unique nor by itself incompatible with the active enlistment of alternative sources of premises, values, and information into the policy process. But during his tenure traditional sources of information—ambassadors and foreign-service officers—played a markedly less significant role, partly because he pre-empted some of their functions as the most widely traveled Secretary of State in history. Moreover, the Dulles-sanctioned "purge" of foreign-service personnel during the zenith of Senator McCarthy's power was a deterrent to accurate reporting by any but the imprudent or the very brave. The severe punishment—loss of careers and often public disgrace —meted out to those who had years earlier warned of difficulties in the Nationalist Government in China did little to encourage frankness in the foreign service. At any rate, there is considerable evidence that the advice of subordinates was neither actively sought, nor, when tendered, was it often of great weight in the making of policy decisions.

Although it is not implied that American foreign policy and the will of John Foster Dulles were identical, a number of factors tended to enlarge the influence of his beliefs on policy decisions. Dulles' conception of his role, buttressed by the consent and support of President Eisenhower, by frequent crises, by the ambiguity of information concerning the Soviet Union, and by his tendency to make decisions with little consultation provided him with wide latitude in the conduct of foreign policy. Consequently, his interpretation of the Soviet Union and its foreign policy assumed considerable importance.

The decision-maker also operates within the somewhat broader and less clearly defined limits delineated by public opinion. In many respects Dulles' attitudes toward the Soviet Union resembled those of the public; opinion surveys have consistently revealed a tendency to view the Soviet Union in black-and-white terms not dissimilar to aspects of Dulles' views. This is not to say, however, that his attitudes merely reflected public opinion. Although public opinion may set broad limits on policy beyond which the decision-maker cannot move, it is also true that public attitudes are in large part shaped by decision-makers.

The role of "educator" was a challenge that Dulles recognized and accepted with characteristic vigor. His distaste for negotiation with the Kremlin derived in part from the fear that Soviet-American agreement on such matters as arms control might have an adverse effect on the public, which could lead to a relaxation of the American defense posture. Yet if his fear of uninformed public opinion was legitimate, his own contribution to its education was often niggardly. Even allowing a generous discount

37

for political partisanship, there was more than a grain of truth in Senator Fulbright's complaint that in respect to the Soviet Union, Dulles "misleads public opinion, confuses it, feeds it pap, tells it that, if it will suppress the proof of its senses, it will see that Soviet triumphs are really defeats and Western defeats are really triumphs."[45] By painting a picture of the world in bold strokes of black and white, interlaced with periodic claims of spectacular American triumphs and calamitous Soviet defeats, he contributed to the latent tendency of the public to view the enemy of the moment in one-dimensional terms.

The extent to which Dulles' assessment of the Soviet Union was correct will become clearer with the passage of time; evaluations of his contemporaries ran from "unerring" to "absurd."[46] Yet some significant errors of judgment, *interpretations that appear to have derived directly from his belief system,* can be identified; these arose not from his "hardheaded" view of Soviet-American differences, but rather from inferences regarding developments in Soviet policy that did not appear to fit the model of an implacable enemy. The situation during the period from 1953 to 1959 was such that any American official would have regarded the Soviet Union as a major threat to the security of the United States; in this respect Dulles' initial premise coincided with those of even his most persistent critics. But no imperative of the situation, role, organization, or public opinion made other aspects of Dulles' beliefs about the Soviet Union inevitable. For example, his premise that Soviet and American interests were in deep conflict on most issues was surely accurate, but whether a similar conflict existed between the Soviet government and the Russian people is open to debate. Certainly, events in the Soviet Union during the years since Dulles' death have produced no evidence to support his conviction. The validity of his view that the Soviet Union possessed the military strength to threaten American security is beyond question, but his prediction that the Soviet system was on the verge of economic collapse—an estimate that contributed to the series of decisions leading to disaster at Suez—remains unfulfilled.

If, as the evidence appears to suggest, at least part of Dulles' attitudes about the Soviet Union can be traced to personal factors, how far can one generalize from these findings? It seems reasonable to suppose that his manner of perceiving and interpreting the environment is not unique among decision-makers. Like Dulles, many Soviet officials have interpreted their

---

[45] Quoted in *The New York Times*, Feb. 8, 1958, 7:2.

[46] *Time*, Vol. XXVI (Feb. 4, 1957), p. 16; Senator Hubert Humphrey, quoted in V. M. Dean, "Two Worlds: Could Both Be True," *Foreign Policy Bulletin*, Vol. XXXV (Mar. 15, 1956), p. 104.

adversaries' actions within a rigid inherent-bad-faith model, that of "monopoly capitalism." Many other examples could be cited. If this premise is correct, the implications for international politics are somewhat sobering.

When decision-makers for both parties to a conflict adhere to rigid images of each other, there is little likelihood that even genuine attempts to resolve the issues will have the desired effect. Such a frame of reference renders meaningful communication with adversaries, much less resolution of the conflict, almost impossible. Even the British, whom Dulles tended to distrust, often found it difficult to get their views across to him by conventional methods: "As a result the British themselves occasionally felt bound to resort to non-diplomatic methods for getting their views across to the Secretary of State; one was to plant them on American secret service agents in the knowledge that they would then get back to Allen Dulles, who would pass them on to his brother, who would take them at their face value."[47] To the extent that each side undeviatingly interprets new information, even conciliatory gestures, in a manner calculated to preserve the original image of the adversary, they are caught up in a closed system with little prospect of changing the relations between them.

Because every decision-maker is in part a prisoner of beliefs and expectations that inevitably shape his definition of reality, to judge Dulles or any individual against a standard of omniscience or total rationality is neither fair nor instructive. Decisions based on less-than-perfect knowledge are unavoidable and will continue to be a source of potential danger as long as foreign policies are formulated by human beings. The avoidable hazards are those that arise from reducing complexities to simplicities, ruling out alternative sources of information and evaluation, and closing off to scrutiny and consideration competing views of reality. On these counts Dulles is open to legitimate criticism.

Modern technology has created an international system in which the potential costs of a foreign policy based on miscalculation have become prohibitive; one of the cruel paradoxes of international politics is that those decisions that require the most serious consideration of alternative interpretations of reality often carry with them the greatest pressures for conformity to stereotyped images. Wisdom in our world consists of maintaining an open mind under such pressures, for a realistic assessment of opportunities and risks in one's relations with adversaries appears to be at least a necessary, if not a sufficient, condition for survival.

[47] Richard Goold-Adams, *The Time of Power: A Reappraisal of John Foster Dulles* (London: Weidenfeld and Nicolson, 1962), p. 309.

REINHOLD NIEBUHR

The Social Myths in the
"Cold War"

Every class and nation defends itself and justifies its interests by a social myth. The myth also is used to detract from the moral prestige of adversaries. Social myths are constructed by imaginative elaborations of actual history. They are hardly ever made out of whole cloth. They arise because reason is more ambiguous in relation to the individual or social self than some rationalists assume. Reason is never the sole master of the acquisitive and anxious self. It is always part master and part servant of that self, particularly the collective self of the nation.

Naturally a social myth must be protected against the criticism of a general community and against competitive myths of competitive collectives in a community. In modern life, the integral national community has the sovereign power and necessary communal consensus to challenge, criticize, and transmute all social myths on the subnational level. But it has neither the inclination nor the power to challenge the mythical content of its own pretensions to virtue that it presents to the larger world, in which neither sovereign power nor consensus exists as a moderating factor upon the self-esteem of nations.

One must analyze this universal character of the mythical nature of all

Reinhold Niebuhr is professor emeritus at Union Theological Seminary in New York City, where he has taught since 1928. He has written numerous articles and books, including *Moral Man and Immoral Society, Nature and Destiny of Man, Christian Realism and Political Problems, The Self and the Dramas of History, The Structure of Nations and Empires,* and *Man's Nature and His Communities.* He is an editor of the bi-weekly *Christianity and Crisis.*

collective self-images and views of the adversary before pointing to the inevitability, but also the error, of the presuppositions of the so-called "free world." There is supposed to be a radical difference between the—supposedly—rational and true approach of the free world to reality, and the noxious myths of the Communist adversary. This adversary gained its political prestige and subsequent economic power on the basis of a most comprehensive myth, rooted in an apocalyptic, semi-religious, and pseudo-scientific program of revolutionary social redemption from all social injustice. Their social presuppositions obviously have a more vivid mythical content than those of the Western democracies. In addition, the Marxist vision of a just society turned out to be a mythical support for a political party that claimed and achieved a monopoly of power, a monopoly necessary to guard the myth from the corroding influence of a free society.

Western democracies assume that the contest between the U.S.S.R.—nation and superpower—and the political forces based on the principle of freedom is indeed an ultimate conflict, probably as ultimate as the Communists, from the viewpoint of their comprehensive myth, declare it to be. Their definition of this conflict, however, contradicts our own definition: it is not a conflict between "freedom" and "tyranny," but between "imperialism" and "democracy."

Before we accept this version of the conflict between free institutions and "tyranny," we must take another precautionary view of the relation of myth to reality. Our review is prompted by a certain apprehension that the advantages of political freedom in discounting myths may have been ignored by the free societies. For the history of their social, political, and economic development does not correspond to either the bourgeois or the proletarian myth. In the modern democratic nation-state the sovereign power was secure enough to allow—through the process of pressure and counter-pressure—the industrial workers to organize, so that the collective power of the trade-unions was set against the collective power of management. Thus, the whole development shows that more than pure reason or conscience was necessary to correct injustices rooted in the mythically pure individualism of the original bourgeois democracy. In other words, it was a tolerable equilibrium of power that produced the free societies.

But is this principle of democratic freedom—so important as a presupposition and indeed as an ingredient in the development of the modern democratic nation-state—applicable or even relevant in the larger arena of international relations? Also, can we expect democratic nations, which have challenged the myth of the messianic class in their own history, to recognize their own mythical pretensions in relation to other nations?

The Social Myths in the "Cold War"

The conflict or the cold war between the Communist world and the free world is described conventionally as the struggle between good and evil, freedom and tyranny, and even as between truth and myth. Yet such distinctions, especially and ironically the last one, themselves partake of the nature of myth. As we have seen, myths are essentially distortions of complex historical events. Undue simplifications of such complexities therefore may be regarded as mythical.

Anti-imperialistic Imperial Superpowers

At this juncture in the world-wide struggle involving men and nations, the two "superpowers," the U.S.S.R. and the U.S., have imperial dimensions and also wield imperial power—economic, political, and military; they surpass, in their impingement upon weaker and client nations, the empires of ancient and medieval eras, as well as the nineteenth-century empires of Europe. Each exercises hegemony in its respective bloc of nations: the U.S. in the non-Communist bloc, and the U.S.S.R. in the more highly integrated Communist empire, consisting of nations that have either opted for the Communist creed or were compelled to accept it by the force of the Russian army.

Although we present ourselves as the leader of the democratic bloc of nations, democracy is only rarely the achievement of the non-Communist nations. More frequently it is either the aspiration or the pretension of the non-Communist nations in our bloc. Naturally our principles prevent us from incorporating the democratic ideal into an explicit imperial structure. The Russians have no such inhibitions; hence we speak polemically, but also accurately, about "Communist imperialism."

It is one of the most vivid ironies of modern history that both these superpowers express ideals of anti-imperialism. The Russians derive their anti-imperialistic idealism and pretension from Marxist dogma and from Lenin's belated amendment to it. According to this dogma, imperialism is the fruit of capitalism, the external expression of the acquisitive impulse that capitalism exhibits in domestic relations. Lenin's amendment to this indictment was borrowed from the English liberal and anti-imperialist J. A. Hobson, whose thesis was simply that the capitalistic quest for markets, raw materials, and investments was accentuated when the capitalist system was in crisis, as it allegedly was.

The Marxist indictment of capitalism was a mythical distortion of an historical fact. All modern European nations used their technical, commercial, and political superiority over the non-technical nations in various expansive, imperialistic movements to extend their dominion. But the motives behind this expansion were complex. They included the pride of power, the exploitative motive of economic profit, and the missionary motive of universalizing moral, political, or technical ideas and values beyond the boundaries of the nation-state. The mythical distortion of the adversary's expansiveness consists simply in singling out the most unacceptable motive, such as the exploitative. A mythical distortion of one's own expansiveness, on the other hand, consists in singling out the missionary motive, rather than the exploitative or power motives. This self-serving shifting of emphasis accounts for that curious phenomenon of an anti-imperialistic Communist imperialism.

Naturally an imperialism rooted in a utopian apocalypse would emphasize its missionary motive. Theoretically, therefore, it desires power for the sake of strategic advantage for the whole "socialist camp." Theoretically, again, it opposes non-Communist nations not because they have free societies, but because they are tainted with "imperialism." Most of the European democratic nations did in fact extend their dominions in Asia and Africa, and their motives were mixed in various proportions. They were usually not as "missionary" as they claimed, whether in behalf of democracy, technical efficiency, or culture. But the relation of Europe to the undeveloped nations was, in fact, not as exploitative as the Communists have claimed. Great Britain, for instance, has been the midwife of autonomous and democratic nations in Asia and Africa, though it must be conceded that the British imperial power bestowed the final grant of freedom because of its own weakness rather than its sense of mission.

We must analyze the imperial impulse and the anti-imperialist pretensions of the Soviet Union in the light of the peculiar history of the Communist apocalypse of social redemption. Designed by Marx for the hoped-for crisis in advanced industrial nations, it instead inspired the revolutionary seizure of power in a traditional, monarchic, and feudal civilization that had collapsed after its defeat in the First World War.

The Russian Revolution, informed by this utopian apocalyptic vision, introduced an economic system that embodied all the Marxist miscalculations. It was ruled by a party that substituted trained revolutionists for Marx's vaguely conceived "dictatorship of the proletariat." The proletariat, marked as the messianic redeemer of all mankind in the original apocalypse, was in fact such a negligible force in the non-technical Russian economy that it could not be a real power in the revolutionary government. But the party, surrogate for the working class in whose name it spoke, turned the tables on the original apocalypse by guiding a non-technical nation to greater technical efficiency.

Two errors contributed to a monopoly of power in the revolutionary consummation. Marx had assumed the supremacy of economic over political power. He also equated the ownership of property with economic power. Thus when the original dream turned into actual history both errors were refuted by this ironic monopoly of economic and political power in the hands of a political party that could dominate the state and also control state-owned property. The party bosses proved the supremacy of political over economic power. Their management of state-owned socialized property proved that ownership of property was not as important as the power of the manager, a fact that has likewise been demonstrated in free societies.

The combination of omnicompetent political bosses and their subordinate managerial oligarchy was ideal for forcing a peasant economy to become technically competent. The government's power over the peasants, once Stalin had collectivized their holdings, enabled it to squeeze capital for industrial investment from this impotent class. Thus Communism, designed to redeem the poor, became in fact an efficient instrument for rapid industrialization at the expense of the poor.

When China, also having a traditional peasant economy with only a nascent industrial sector, copied the Russian revolutionary model, it became quite clear that a nation of politically and economically impotent peasants could not challenge the monopoly of party power, and that the nation actually would profit from such a monopoly.

The contradiction between the apocalyptic dreams and myths and the post-revolutionary power realities was thus not a hindrance, but an aid, to the expansion of Communist power in the non-technical world. In contrast, the workers in Western democracies had the freedom to challenge the contradiction between myths and post-revolutionary reality. They also had the means, within the shifting equilibria of a fluid economy, to set collective power against the collective power of management. The Western industrial workers therefore never were as desperate as the Marxist myth assumed. Even though bourgeois democracy was slow to discount and correct the original bourgeois individualistic myths, Western democracies proved themselves immune to the Communist virus. The Communist myth evidently was plausible in the non-technical world but irrelevant in the advanced nations of the West, where political freedom had been established before the development of modern industry.

This contrast between the Communism of the non-technical cultures and the capitalism and democracy of the West throws light on our subordinate thesis that the sovereign power of free nations is able to refute the myths of its sub-national groups and classes, not only because a free society gives all classes the opportunity to criticize and challenge the claims and pretensions of its competitors and allies, but also because the sovereign authority of a relatively neutral state, whose authority transcends the prestige of all classes, is able to change an equilibrium of power for the sake of tolerable justice and in favor of a comparatively powerless class.

It was this achievement of free societies in Western Europe that refuted the Marxist apocalypse of doom. For the individually impotent workers, who were robbed both of their skills and of their tools by the modern power machines, were given the right to organize and bargain collectively, and thus to construct a new equilibrium of power that has established a situation of tolerable economic justice in all Western industrial, democratic states. Thus the old, irrelevant individualistic competition, which exposed the workers to the competitions of a market economy in the realm of labor, was gradually transmuted into the modern "welfare state."

It would be idle and dangerous to obscure the great contrast between domestic economies and cultures, between free societies and those governed by political oligarchies inspired by the Marxist myth, a myth shielded from scrutiny by the oligarchies' monopoly of power. But it would be foolish to assume that this contrast between the two systems would be pertinent to an analysis of the mythical statements of foreign policy by which both systems present their pretensions to the outside world.

The U.S. and the U.S.S.R., which exercise hegemony over the so-called "free world" and "socialist camp" respectively, accuse each other of imperialism. We speak of "Communist imperialism" for the simple reason that the Communist myth sanctions a supranational imperial structure. The Communists accuse us of imperialism simply because their myth defines imperialism as the ultimate fruit of capitalism. Are we not, therefore, imperialists, despite our avowal of innocence?

There are, of course, differences in the myths by which each nation avows its innocence. We have previously defined the apocalyptic myth of Communism. Our myth of innocence may be described as "nostalgic." John Locke, rather than Marx, was the source of a liberal democratic universalism and anti-imperialism. Locke wrote: "The end of government is the good of mankind, and which is best for mankind: that the people should be always exposed to the boundless will of tyranny, or that the rulers should be sometimes liable to be opposed when they grow exorbitant in the use of their power . . . ?"[1] Our founding fathers regarded our nation

[1] John Locke, *Two Treatises of Government*, ed. by J. W. Gough (Oxford: Basil Blackwell, 1946), *Second Treatise*, Chap. XIX, par. 229.

as innocent because of our war of independence against an imperial power. This sense of innocence was preserved in spite of our development and growth to mature strength for the simple reason that our hemispheric economic expanse made classical imperialism unnecessary.

Thomas Jefferson was probably the first of a long line of American liberal democratic anti-imperialists to equate democracy with an ideal of universalism. He wrote in 1820: "We exist and are quoted as standing proof, that a government so modelled as to rest continually on the whole of society, is a practical government . . . . As members therefore of the universal society of mankind, and as standing in a high and responsible relation to them, it is our sacred duty not to blast the confidence we have inspired of proof that a government based on reason is better than one based on force."[2]

The most explicit expression of America's sense of messianic mission was Woodrow Wilson's address in 1916 before we entered the First World War. Wilson said then: "We are holding off, not because we do not feel concerned, but because when we exert the force of this nation we want to know what we are exerting it for. We ought to have a touchstone . . . that it is truly American, that the States of America are set up to vindicate the rights of man against the rights of property, or the rights of self-aggrandizement and aggression. . . . When you are asked, 'Aren't you willing to fight?' answer yes, you are waiting for something worth fighting for."[3]

When our nation became darkly conscious of the fact that our peace and security were dependent upon the British navy and that a German victory would imperil British control of the sea, unrestricted submarine warfare gave us a moral excuse for entering a conflict that an idealistic nation, unconscious of its normal impulses of survival, was hesitant to enter. Wilson was again in perfect accord with the American sense of messianic mission when he projected a moral goal for the conflict we had entered. It was a "war to make the world safe for democracy."

The Wilsonian doctrine was an ideal moral fig leaf for a messianic nation in its first encounter with the problems of a nascent imperial dimension of power. He gave an additional buttress to our self-image as a pure nation by projecting the "League of Nations" as the ultimate end of the conflict. This goal would substantiate our moral reasons for engaging in the conflict and refute criticism that we were motivated by self-aggrandizement. Need-

[2] *The Writings of Thomas Jefferson*, ed. by Andrew A. Lipscomb and Albert E. Bergh (Washington, D. C.: Thomas Jefferson Memorial Assn., 1904), Vol. XV, p. 285.
[3] Quoted in Edward Buehrig, *Woodrow Wilson and the Balance of Power* (Bloomington: Indiana University Press, 1956), pp. 247-48.

less to say, the League was rejected by the nation that proposed it, partly because the draconic peace of Versailles offended our perfectionists, and partly because our self-regarding patriots thought the League provided inadequate security for our national interests. The moral of the Wilsonian adventure in world politics might be that it is as difficult for a messianic democratic nation as it is for a Communist one to veil the hiatus between myth and reality in international relations.

If there is any consistent line between Jefferson's and Wilson's mythical images of the purity of American international goals, it may be significant that many aspects of our foreign policy between Jefferson and Wilson were conveniently forgotten in our search for a plausible myth of national purity. Two intervening chapters of our national history must be recalled to measure the capacity for self-deception, even on the part of democratic nations, in projecting mythical self-images to the world.

One chapter consists of our expansion in this hemisphere immediately after our birth as a sovereign nation. That expansion challenged all other sovereignties in the hemisphere with the threat of war, or with war itself (as in our acquisition of Texas from Mexico). This imperial or expansive movement was undertaken under the slogan of "Manifest Destiny." In short, it vividly revealed the inclination to express expansive policies in the name of an ideal that explicitly denied the legitimacy of expansion. "Manifest Destiny" merely affirmed that a democratic nation was "destined" to occupy a hemisphere because the purity of its democratic ideals would justify this expansion. Yet this very expansion was obviously in conflict with the ideal used to justify this inevitable imperial impulse of a growing nation. The expansiveness of "Manifest Destiny" was thus a vivid revelation of the fact that nations, as individuals, tend to deceive themselves when they project a self-image to the world that obscures the dominant motives of foreign policy. Thus, the less acceptable expansive impulse of the nation is given the cover of professed moral or "democratic" purpose.

Wilson's conviction that our nation was "the most unselfish nation in history" evidently was informed by a mythical sense of virtue, which must have ignored a second chapter of our national history. This chapter is the record of our venture in overt, rather than covert, imperialism. Because it was prompted by Spain's attempt to enforce her imperial sovereignty over a rebellious Cuban colony, there was some substance to our moral pretext for challenging Spain in a war that gave us the booty of the entire Spanish imperial domain in the Caribbean and Pacific.

Naturally our traditional anti-imperialism made it difficult for us to swallow the colonial morsels suddenly placed before us. The anti-imperialist conscience of a nation that had never before embarked on an overtly imperialist venture was eloquently expressed by Senator Hoar of Massachusetts. Our founding fathers, said the Senator, ". . . would have never betrayed these sacred and awful verities, that they might strut about in the castoff clothing of pinchbek emperors and pewter kings."[4]

President McKinley—a Republican whose Vice-President was none other than "Rough Rider" Theodore Roosevelt, one of the many heroes of our new imperialism—was sufficiently under the influence of our anti-imperialistic myth of national innocence to have qualms of conscience about our acquisition of the Philippines. He reported that these qualms were eased by a dream in which he received the inspiration that "We keep the Philippines, evangelize, Christianize and educate them."[5] Significantly, the dream contained the myth of national purity in a nutshell.

But these moral qualms also resulted in an ambivalence, of which the Platt Amendment to the treaty with Spain was a significant, though dubious, fruit. The Platt Amendment disavowed any territorial ambitions in regard to Cuba, though it reserved our right to maintain a naval base there. This abnegation of overt imperialism in regard to Cuba might be considered dubious because it was irresponsible. In this respect, it was in marked contrast to our policy in the Philippines. While we were gradually creating the resources of autonomous nationhood and democracy in the Philippines, Cuba, though politically free, was being exploited by economic imperialists and ruled by one corrupt dictatorship after another, until it finally fell prey to the revolutionary movement led by Fidel Castro.

The difference between the destiny of Cuba and that of the Philippines might instruct us about the virtues of a responsible imperial sense of mission, and the weaknesses of an irresponsible, covert, usually economic imperialism that is devoid of any sense of obligation for guiding new nations to a viable national independence and democratic government.

The myth of our innocence, that we were untainted by imperial expansiveness, was maintained despite our growth in economic power, because of our continental economy. Thus, despite our power, size, and wealth, we continued to be anti-imperialistic. Accordingly, we were able to criticize the empires even of our democratic allies in Europe.

The embarrassment to our allies over our self-righteousness must have been particularly acute in the case of Britain. The intimate friendship between President Roosevelt and Winston Churchill, and the effective

[4] Quoted in George Kennan, *American Diplomacy, 1900-1950* (Chicago: Chicago University Press, 1952), p. 16.
[5] *Ibid.*, p. 18.

alliance between the two Anglo-Saxon democracies could not overcome our sense of superior virtue, even when the anti-Nazi alliance of Britain, America, and Russia yielded so much evidence that our affinities with Britain were stronger than those with Communist Russia. Although President Roosevelt regarded his occasional siding with Stalin as an important stratagem of peace, it may have been partly prompted by the feeling that the British, tainted as they were by imperialism, were unworthy of our wholehearted cooperation.[6]

In the days before the "cold war," it was taken for granted that the U.S. and U.S.S.R. shared a common tradition of anti-imperialism. Thus General Eisenhower could write in 1948: "The past relations between America and Russia were no cause to regard the future with pessimism. Historically the two nations had preserved an unbroken friendship, dating back to the birth of the United States as an independent Republic . . . . Both were free of the stigma of empire-building by force."[7]

Though the General was not an historian, he could not possibly have intended to absolve the old Russian empire of the guilt of "empire-building by force." One can only view this remarkable statement of Russo-American affinity as indicating the author's sense of the similarity between the Communist and our own pretensions to anti-imperial virtue. Even so, the statement is rather startling in the light of subsequent history. Mr. Eisenhower could not foresee that the Communist ideology would become the cement holding together a multi-national empire; that it would overcome the anti-Russian resentments of the subordinate nations, such as the Ukraine; and that it would provide the sense of a common cause, superior to the ideology of the Orthodox Church, by which the Islamic Asiatic republics could be integrated into an imperial nation. Even the conquest of the Eastern European satellite nations ultimately would be defended by an appeal to the validity of the Communist mythical universalism.

It is somewhat ironic now to recall this American recognition of a shared anti-imperialism, for the cold war meanwhile has seen each nation intensify its criticism of the other's myths. Russia, in the context of its own myth, was the holy land of the new religion of Communism, destined to redeem mankind from all capitalistic and imperialistic injustices. But she is regarded by all the nations of the "free world" as the hegemonial power of a new imperialism; and not without reason, for the Communist

[6] See Herbert Feis, *Roosevelt, Churchill, Stalin: The War They Waged and the Peace They Sought* (Princeton: Princeton University Press, 1957), particularly p. 574.
[7] Dwight D. Eisenhower, *Crusade in Europe* (New York: Doubleday and Co., Inc., 1948), p. 457.

myth ordained the supranational economic integration of all Communist nations.

The Communists saw this supranational integration as nothing but a "fraternal" relationship between the holy land of the new religion and all the smaller, often non-technical, nations. According to the Communist myth, there are no power rivalries in the "socialist camp." They were all eliminated by the elimination of the source of all evil: property. With the socialization of property, the world obviously must experience a new reality in which power rivalries would no longer figure in the relationship of strong and weak nations.

Naturally that part of the world not influenced by Communist mythology saw the imperial realities rather than the Communist rationalization of them. But the Communist indictment of all imperialism except its own had a particular effect upon the United States. We were, according to the Communist myth, the leader of the imperialistic nations, because we were the most powerful of the "capitalistic" nations. Naturally we were outraged; for was there not, at least among our utopians, an original conviction that both the U.S. and the U.S.S.R. were innocent of the charge of "empire-building by force"?

Perhaps the fervor of our anti-Communism was partly prompted by the divergence and contradiction between these two myths of world redemption. Ironies were compounded when historical providence made our innocent American democracy into one of the two imperial nations. Common sense certainly suggests that there were similar imperialistic impulses in both these powerful nations. But since both were by definition innocent of these impulses according to their own myths, both continued to proclaim their respective innocence. At the same time, the differences in their myths prompted them to cast each other in the role of the devil. We, as well as the Russians, are incapable of correcting or modifying our own national myths. Thus modern history is fated to be governed by two contrasting myths of the two superpowers, one of which uses the injustices of early-nineteenth-century European industrialism to prove its indictment of capitalism, long after these injustices have been corrected by the new equilibria of power perfected by the free nations.

But even our own imperial nation, though democratic, finds it hard to revise the charge against "Communist tyranny," even though a decade has elapsed since the Twentieth Party Congress, under Khrushchev's leadership, revealed the capacity of the oligarchies of a managerial society to take steps to protect themselves from the cruel despotism of a Stalin. This new development did not herald, as some optimists hoped, the gradual emergence of democratic institutions. Russia remained a managerial political society. But the "free world" did not adjust the language of its popular indictments of "Communist despotism" in accordance with these developments, though our experts and learned men discussed them in detail.

The Myth of Democratic Universality

In analyzing the capacity of the two superpowers to become hegemonial in their respective alliance systems, it becomes apparent that each nation tends to universalize its own domestic achievement. Democracy, for example, is regarded by many as universally desirable and applicable. But since democracy is an achievement that requires cultural, technical, and other capacities on the part of a population, it may be a political myth to regard the democratic achievement as a possibility for all cultures and economies. Historical evidence shows that only a few nations of Western Europe had the necessary homogeneity, educational level, and political skill to make the democratic principle of "authority by consent of the governed" workable.

Our own superpower is inclined to regard democracy as a universal option for all nations. We are inclined toward this democratic utopianism because of our unique history. We built our nation on a virgin continent that lacked all the problems which European nations had to surmount before free governments became viable. Although we did not have the ethnic and religious homogeneity that proved so important a precondition of free governments in Europe, we did have one language; and our hemispheric expanse made it possible for us to scatter our immigrant population so that no one language or race was localized. Great Britain, in contrast, did not absorb its Gaelic minorities in Wales and Scotland in one step. First Henry VII brought England and Wales under a single sovereignty. Then, when James VI of Scotland became the legitimate heir of Queen Elizabeth, he became James I of England and Scotland. Naturally the unification under royal auspices was solidified by centuries of cultural integration and the remarkable political and religious accommodation of the Elizabethan settlement. The sovereign being the Defender of the Faith and head of the Church, this meant that the monarch was Anglican in England and Presbyterian in Scotland.

This shrewd contrivance shows how ethnic diversity was compounded when identical with religious diversity; for religious loyalties tend to give a more ultimate dimension to other ethnic or linguistic loyalties and diversities. The nations of Europe suffered from religious wars for centuries after the Reformation. Our own nation, religiously the most pluralistic of any Western nation, found the secret of making this religious pluralism a resource, rather than an obstacle, for the unity of the nation. The secret was a rigorous separation of church and state, which helped to secure the loyalty of the most diverse groups to the national community. But our nation alone possessed the prerequisite for the rigorous separation of church and state: the absence of any religious group so dominant that it would oppose this religious neutrality.

Most of the democratic nations of the West could not validate their free societies until they had come to terms with the problems of modern industrialism, and proved that it was possible for a free society to grant political and economic power to the industrial workers. Though our nation had the usual maladjustments, social protests, and ferments—showing that even liberal democracies required a century to come to terms with the social and economic problems of modern industry—we were fortunate, being a purely bourgeois culture without a feudal background, that modern injustices were not superimposed on feudal class resentments. The Marxist rebellion did not appeal to our workers, despite their early resentments as powerless individuals in a collectivist economy. We were therefore unconscious of the many stages of social adjustment that a free society must undergo before it can validate itself. In the economic realm, as well as in problems of ethnic or religious diversity, our own superpower was therefore tempted to regard free institutions as more easily achieved than Western history has proved them to be. Hence our tendency to project our free institutions as world-wide options.

There is much evidence, however, that our failure to consider the obstacles posed by ethnic, linguistic, and cultural diversity to the establishment of free societies makes our projection of democracy as viable for all nations somewhat of a utopian myth. India, for example, is troubled by many economic problems in negotiating an entrance into modern industrial civilization. But her linguistic and cultural diversity, as revealed by her recent language riots, also threatens her democratic order. India availed herself of the English language of her former masters; but the universal use of English is strictly provisional. Once the educational process of a new generation, lacking competence in English, has run its course, the unity of India under free institutions may well be imperilled.

The new nations of Africa all have problems of linguistic and tribal diversity, stemming from their primitive past. The difficulties in establishing either unity or democracy in the Congo are well known. But the Congo was notoriously unprepared for either independence or democracy;

therefore the tribal chaos, from which even a United Nations intervention failed to rescue her, cannot be regarded as typical.

Nigeria, on the other hand, was scrupulously prepared by her colonial masters for both autonomy and democracy. But she lacked political parties that transcended the confines of her three regions. The Islamic northern region was politically integrated compared with the other two regions of the Yorubas and the Ebos. Her first federal Prime Minister, Balewa, was a symbol of the political power of the Islamic northern region. A bloody military revolt, initiated by the two southern regions, resulted in the death of Balewa and the abolition of the democratic institutions so carefully nurtured by the British. The situation, which is still in flux, may well illustrate the problem of building democratic institutions when confronted with tribal, regional, and religious diversity.

Clearly the problem of diversity, which we in this country were able to solve because of very favorable circumstances, is a tremendous hindrance to the growth of free institutions in Africa. We often seem to forget that the democracies of Europe evolved free institutions during centuries of pre-democratic triumphs over the diversities of language, religion, and race, usually under the auspices of royal sovereignty. Therefore, we must not regard free institutions as viable instruments of national unity in Africa in the immediate future. Presented to the new nations as a universally applicable alternative, democracy takes on the qualities of a utopian myth.

Fortunately, the Communist myth of redemption has even less credibility than our utopian democratic myth, since the African nations lacked the feudal background that made the Communist myth credible in European or Asiatic economic conditions. Conditions in Africa are more favorable for a socialist economy, which would bring all economic processes under political authority.

Advantages and Disadvantages of the Two Myths

We have been comparing the myths and realities in the contest between the Soviet Union and the United States, both of whom have power of imperial dimensions and foreign policies informed by myths. This comparison must conclude with an analysis of the advantages and disadvantages that these two hegemonial nations derive in their contest from the fact that the Communist myth sanctions an imperial structure, whereas our democratic ideology does not sanction any policy that challenges the sovereignty or pride of any independent nation.

In an era in which pride of national autonomy is the main concern of both old and new nations, the Communist myth is an embarrassment to the Soviets. It obviously offends the national pride of the old nations of Eastern Europe. Since the Hungarian uprising in 1956, the European satellites have been increasingly restive under the yoke of Soviet imperialism. China, whose size alone would cause her to resent Soviet hegemony, has in fact invented a new Communist myth that challenges Moscow's imperial authority, particularly its claim to be the authoritative interpreter of the Communist dogma. The inclination and capacity for inventing a new myth, which makes the Russian version guilty of "revisionist" heresy and China the real authority on revolutionary orthodoxy, is in fact a clear indication that powerful nations can and do revise their imperial myths when the original myth is in contradiction with the national interest.

Russia is both white and technically competent, and therefore affluent. China is both colored and poor. It was almost inevitable that she would be tempted to revise the myth in terms that would suit her national interests, rather than those of Russia. Russia has no national interest in exporting revolution, though there must be many Russian devotees of the original Marxist myth. In any case, there must be many more who know that Russia's national interests will not be enhanced by risking her new affluence in courting a nuclear war. With China, on the other hand, there is a perfect conjunction between national pride and the prospective world-wide revolution of the poor and colored nations. Thus, there are two Communist imperial nations competing with each other for prestige among the Communist parties of Asia and Africa. It must be very disconcerting to the old believers in the original Marxist dogma.

Our concern for the independent nation, on the other hand, gives us a tremendous advantage in a day in which budding nations in Asia and Africa are jealous of their freedom and suspicious of any imperial pretensions. Military revolts against Ben Bella in Algeria, Nkrumah in Ghana, and Sukarno in Indonesia were all prompted by the armies' patriotic concern that these revolutionary political dictators were too subservient to the imperial interests of Communist imperial nations.

But our satisfaction over this advantage must not obscure the tremendous political problem of honesty that a nation like ours faces when it is challenged to use its military force in pursuing its hegemonial responsibilities. The average voter knows little and cares less about these imperial responsibilities, such as assuring the safety of the non-Communist nations on the fringes of Asia, but is moved only by appeals to our common democratic idealism, which usually is informed by a static anti-Communism. Our engagement in Vietnam has consequently forced the Administration to create a series of obvious fictions or myths calculated to obscure the hiatus between our idealism and our hegemonial responsibilities.

The hiatus is obscured by resorting to the previously analyzed myth of projecting national self-determination as a universal possibility for all cultures. Our military presence is needed to guarantee the security of the non-Communist nations on the fringe of Asia. Our air bases in Thailand ensure the presence of our military power. But we also need a harbor for our ships. That indicates Vietnam as the locus for our presence. Very well, we will invite ourselves to defend the "right of self-determination" for the southern half of the partitioned nation. President Johnson and Secretary Rusk are very Wilsonian in their idealism, and, accordingly, we are told that we are only protecting a small nation from the "aggression" of its neighbors.

Unfortunately, these myths and pretensions of our foreign policy are not sufficiently credible to obscure our real hegemonial purposes. None of the three small nations of Indochina seems capable either of integral nation-hood or of self-government. Their peasant cultures lack both the techni-cal and cultural prerequisites for Western-style democracy. When the Geneva Conference picked up the pieces of the fallen French empire in Indochina, only Vietnam was partitioned. The other two nations, Laos and Cambodia, were neutralized. Vietnam was partitioned because it con-tained a group of Catholic anti-Communists, who moved to the non-Communist South.

We were originally sucked into this vacuum in Indochina by the offer of financial help and "military advisers." Our aid has since grown to astronomical proportions, including billions of dollars and thousands of American lives. Our original fictional justification was that we were defend-ing a democracy. But when the Diem regime was toppled by a bloody army revolt, this fiction was exposed by the obvious realities. The American expenditure of money and blood has increased, though South Vietnam is now obviously governed by a series of army juntas who have difficulty acquiring not only the fig leaf of constitutional government, but also the control of many of the villages over which they claim to exercise sover-eignty.

One of the many reasons why this large commitment of an affluent nation has not been more successful is that the leader of North Vietnam is the legendary Communist boss and national patriot, Ho Chi Minh, who is regarded by the peasants as the father of his country, that is, the whole of Vietnam. He has the aura of a national patriot because he led the successful revolt against the French colonial masters. Ironically, in his estimation we are merely the successors of the French imperialists, whereas according to our own democratic myth, we are the big brother of all weak nations.

The public reaction to this essentially unpopular war is compounded of various motives. The idealistic democratic myth is important for many voters. On the other hand, the fear that our prestige as an imperial nation may suffer if the Communists make our position untenable influences many members of Congress. Despite the negative attitude of most of our university scholars and experts, an attitude supported by many Church leaders and journalists, a shifting proportion of the public, and probably most of the military, support the war effort because they fear an ultimate military conflict with Red China for which our foothold on the peninsula is alleged to be a strategic advantage. Thus the confusion of myths—involving problems of prestige and power—and the fears of a conflict with a dominant power in Asia hold a great democratic nation in the grip of a pitiless commitment.

Whether it is feasible, necessary, or even possible to challenge a great Asian power by military force remains an unexplored question. Undoubtedly we have given additional evidence for the old saying that foreign affairs is the Achilles' heel of democracy. The myths underlying our foreign policy seem to lead an open society into confusion.

The Secretary-General of the United Nations, U Thant, gave the verdict of an uncommitted observer on this strange and awful mythical struggle in the little nation of Vietnam: "I see nothing but danger in the idea, so assiduously cultivated outside Vietnam, that this conflict is a kind of holy war between two powerful political ideologies."

STANLEY HOFFMANN

Perceptions, Reality, and the Franco-American Conflict

I

The distinction between perception and reality in world politics is always arbitrary. Here as elsewhere, perceptions are part of reality. The student of politics who looks only at patterns of behavior but leaves out the meanings that the actors give to their own and to each other's conduct turns into a specialist of shadows. Taken as a whole, international politics is a set of trends that are often compelling to the actors even if they do not perceive or understand those trends correctly, and a set of perceptions that shape policies. For perceptions are more than a part of political reality: they mold it, insofar as they are the springs and fuel of action. Moreover, they are themselves shaped by reality.

The problem of perception vs. reality arises nevertheless for two important reasons. In the first place, the perceptions of each actor are shaped by his own experience, by a segment of reality which is not the same as that which matters to and moves other actors; the actors' attempts to shape reality project onto the world stage those different experiences and segments. Distortions and conflicts are thus ensured by the selectiveness and parochialism of perceptions. Second, the compelling objective trends account for only a part of world affairs. The international system, although

Stanley Hoffmann is professor of government at Harvard University, where he is associated with the Center for International Affairs. In addition to numerous articles in scholarly journals here and abroad, he is the author of *Contemporary Theory in International Relations* and *The State of War*, and a co-author of *In Search of France*.

it imposes certain limits and imperatives on the policies of the actors, is largely the outcome of their decisions and operations. The basic trends are often malleable enough to be twisted or even reversed by the main actors' moves. Thus, reality is in considerable part the product of a conflict of wills, of a contest of active perceptions competing for the privilege of defining reality. As long as the test is unresolved, each contender has, so to speak, his own reality; "real" reality is still in the making, more obscure than the clashing perceptions. Once the test is over, reality marks either the point of equilibrium reached by deadlocked wills, or the scope of the triumph of the prevailing will; retrospectively, the perceptions that lost will now appear to the observer as having deviated from reality.

Thus the uncertainty, complexity, and openness of the international system account for the importance of the creative role of perceptions and for the difficulty of determining before the end of the game which perceptions have more weight and efficiency. This importance and this difficulty in turn contribute to the fundamental uncertainty of world politics. The role of perceptions has become even more essential in the postwar international system, again for two reasons.

First, the present system undermines and transforms many of the generally accepted components of "reality" in world affairs. Whereas it had been widely recognized that there existed a high correlation between a state's material ingredients of power and its capacity to reach its goals, the new conditions of the use of force and the spread of what one might call the legitimacy of the nation-state have lowered that correlation, tended to equalize the actors, and made the evaluation of power infinitely more complex. The purely objective ingredients are more difficult to translate into effective results, and the more subjective ones have gained more weight: a correct perception of other actors' goals and handicaps, and of the limits within which maneuver is possible can become a partial substitute for material power. When the physics of power declines, the psychology of power rises. Also, reality was usually defined in terms of who controlled what and who possessed what. The same new factors have led states to transfer their greed and expectations from physical mastery to the shaping of the international milieu—from tangibles to intangibles. What constitutes success and failure in such a quest, what is "real" gain, or merely "symbolic" or "illusionary" achievement is hard to say. Again, much depends on perceptions. Perhaps international politics today should be defined less as a struggle for power than as a contest for the shaping of perceptions. When force loses some of its prominence, power—my exercise of control over you—becomes the art of making you see the world the way

I see it, and of making you behave in accordance with that vision. International politics in the past was often an arena of coercion without persuasion; it is tending to become an arena of persuasion, more or less coercive.

In the second place, the importance of perceptions in a system where the less powerful actors have acquired new leverage is further boosted by the increase in the number of actors. When the skills of persuasion have to be spread over so many players, the uncertainty of the game—to use a most fashionable term—escalates. Reality becomes the game, but the outcome remains clouded. Since every actor's perception of himself, of others, and of the game is shaped by his national situation, the gaps in perception, the divergences, and the conflicts multiply; any one power's ability to shape the milieu by molding the perceptions consequently decreases.

II

The Franco-American conflict of recent years is a fascinating example of the importance of perceptions. Both countries (i.e., the statesmen in charge of foreign affairs) start with the same notion of reality; but the agreement is so narrow as to be almost meaningless, for what is obvious to both is far less significant than what is at issue. What is obvious to both is (1) the existence of a struggle between two superpowers, one of whose main stakes is the control of Western Europe; (2) the decline of Western Europe's influence because of the events of the 1930's and of World War II; (3) the present necessity for Western Europe to seek military security in an alliance with the United States; (4) the imperative of managing the struggle in such a way as to avoid a nuclear war; and (5) the existence of an irresistible tide of decolonization (a fact the French were slow in recognizing). This constitutes reality for both, and yet there is a serious clash of perceptions about reality owing to conflicting visions of international affairs and conflicting diplomatic styles. Those visions and styles, the perceptions that underlie them and which they in turn inspire, and the foreign policies that follow are in the final analysis the products of different pasts, different positions, and different procedures.

Images of World Politics

Since 1947 there has been one dominant American image of international affairs, and of America's role in them. World politics has been seen as a contest pitting the forces of order, stability, and evolutionary change against the forces of aggression and subversion. The role of the former is

59

to contain the latter in such a way that statesmen with an evil intent will not only find their enterprises thwarted, but also conclude that it is in their own best interest to mend their ways and to play a responsible, i.e., non-violent, part in the global symphony. The role of the forces of order also consists of encouraging everywhere those political leaders and groups that stand for moderation. The shapers of American policy perceive the United States as being, both by necessity and by vocation, the one nation that carries world responsibilities in this battle for order. Only the U.S. has the combination of power, values, institutions, and interests that makes for leadership all over the globe. This is not to say that they consider the U.S. to be a "global policeman" protecting its own narrow interests. American leaders, while obviously looking after those interests, nevertheless perceive the interest of mankind as identical to the higher interest of the U.S.; they see in the U.S. the secular arm of an ideal that is of universal value (even to the foes who still refuse to see the light and whose actions, if left unchecked, would only breed chaos); they consider America's involvement to be a necessary and proper substitute for the frequent failure of other nations to share the burden.

Three elements of this image are especially relevant to the Franco-American crisis. First, the American view of international affairs encompasses both the notion of a duel between two groups—one might call it a contest between black and white—and the idea of ultimate, if hard won, harmony. Second, such a view provides the U.S. with an apparently simple criterion for evaluating other nations' behavior: they will be in or out of favor depending on whether their performance contributes to or detracts from the efforts to build an effective common barrier against the forces of disorder, on whether their acts advance or retard the attainment of ultimate harmony. Third, there is in the American approach what might be called an attitude of selfless superiority: superiority because of a deep conviction that the American sense of purpose and responsibility provides U.S. foreign policy with a yardstick for the calculation of everyone's best interest; selfless because the yardstick is used for a conception of the common rather than the purely American good.

French perceptions of international affairs clash with America's at every point. French leaders—and especially de Gaulle—see world politics as a *multiple* contest in which efforts at dividing the contenders into two camps are both dangerous and futile: dangerous because such a division threatens peace as well as the independence of the weaker actors; futile because it is of the essence of the international milieu that ideological camps and military coalitions disintegrate under the strains of rival national interests. As a result, any expectation of final harmony is deemed naïve: the range of choices is instead a gamut of grays, extending from bellicose instability to fragile moderation. In such a world, the French expect the dominant power(s) to seek to preserve and extend their sway, and to rationalize or disguise it—either in order to deceive others or through self-deception—under a cloak of ideological messianism or altruistic universality. As for the smaller powers, though they may have no choice but to seek the protection of a giant, their interest and therefore their duty is thought to be in maintaining a margin of autonomy in order to preserve their own integrity and self-respect, and to safeguard a chance of restoring a system of world order that will moderate the clashes and balance the claims of the great.

Hence there is a wide gap between the perceptions of the two nations in two important areas. On the one hand, American leaders (and many scholars as well) believe that international politics in the nuclear age would be least stable if the number of major actors pursuing their national interests in traditional ways increased too much, and most stable if the two superpowers should prove capable of overcoming their antagonisms and of pooling, so to speak, their responsibilities *qua* great powers: for such a duopoly would be tantamount to a conversion of the Soviets to America's notion of order. To the French, such Soviet-American cooperation would perhaps ensure peace and stability at the strategic level, but it would also impose intolerable restraints on smaller powers; in particular, it would probably consolidate the partition of Europe and preserve the *de facto* hegemony of each superpower in "its" half of Europe.

Images of Each Other

On the other hand, there is also an interesting contrast in the two nations' perceptions of each other. The United States judges French actions under de Gaulle as wicked because it measures them against the kind of world order it deems of interest to humanity. The French attacks on and secession from NATO are perceived as dangerous for Western security, as giving aid and comfort to the forces of chaos. The French nuclear arsenal is considered wasteful and an encouragement to irresponsibility. French nationalism is resented as being anachronistic (in the age of giants no state with the size and resources of France can aspire to a "real" role), nefarious (it could be contagious), and destructive (it has brought to a jarring halt the postwar efforts for West European integration and the development of an Atlantic partnership). French attacks on the dollar, demands for a return to the gold standard, and conversions of dollars into gold are dismissed as absurd and mischievous.

Perceptions, Reality, and the Franco-American Conflict

In other words, given its own viewpoint and criteria, the United States perceives French foreign policy as the capricious, if systematic, demolition of all that seemed promising in postwar Western policy. When Mr. Bowie calls de Gaulle a tragic figure, he expresses this perception aptly. And yet although the perception of the immediate impact and effect of de Gaulle's acts is correct, there is a misperception of his purposes. American officials and commentators tend to see in his moves only an "atavistic" nationalism, to use Dean Acheson's words, a desire to bring back the world of 1913. They fail, in my opinion, to understand that his vision of a French return to "grandeur" is inseparable from his vision of a new international system that, though multipolar, would nevertheless differ profoundly from the world of the nineteenth century precisely because of the restraints imposed by nuclear weapons, of the emergence of many new independent states, and of the cooperative functional ties among nations. Nor do American experts, blinded by what de Gaulle's acts have done to Monnet's dream, perceive the European patriotism of de Gaulle, which may be obscured by his hatred of supranationality, but which even explains some of this hatred. In his view a supranational Europe at this stage of history would be incapable of having any true identity of its own.

If American misperceptions of France result largely from an implicit conviction that the best a smaller Western power can hope to do is to occupy the rather modest seat assigned to it in the "grand design," French misperceptions of American policy are of a slightly different nature. On the whole, French observers also apply to the U.S. a set of preconceived notions. These are not the notions of what an orderly world *ought* to be, but rather the notions of how a major power *tends* to behave. Americans criticize France for departing from a yardstick France does not *want* to observe; the French criticize the U.S. for behaving in a way that Americans quite indignantly deny *is* their mode of behavior. What Americans resent about French actions is their impact on the American design: de Gaulle's vision is half misunderstood, half rejected. Although, in my opinion, what is involved is partly a misperception of de Gaulle's intentions, this does not matter too much to the French, partly because the style of Gaullist (and indeed classical European) diplomacy is rather indifferent to motives and intentions, partly because the bulk of the American criticism deals with the "consequences of General de Gaulle." On the contrary, France's quarrel with the U.S. is a quarrel about motives: the French are convinced that the U.S. acts as a hegemonial nation, slightly drunk with power, and resorts like all empires to moralistic window dressing of the naked *animus dominandi*. As a result, there is an occasional tendency to misperceive the consequences of American acts—for instance by expecting, all too logically, American interventionism to be universal. But the main emphasis is on motivations. Americans, faced with French acts, bemoan their impact. The French, faced with American acts, waste little time deploring their impact because they expect great powers to act that way, i.e., to try to preserve their privileged position by rewarding the most docile and by opposing the most rebellious of their allies, to try to reach agreements with each other behind the backs of weaker partners, to use force in the defense of threatened positions, etc. Nothing could be more resented in the United States. For what is attacked, it is felt here, is the very integrity of America's policy, not merely its results; Americans denounce French moves, the French attack America's self-image. The United States blames France for departing from the only "reality": a modest place within an integrated framework. At least both sides agree that France has indeed rejected that framework, an agreement that makes relatively dispassionate discussion possible. The French perceive the Americans as behaving according to the only reality: the struggle for power. As a result, the debate becomes both acrimonious and elusive. It is acrimonious because the Americans feel unfairly blamed and insulted, even though the French attitude is far more cynical than sanctimonious. In effect the French are saying, "Now it's your turn to behave that way, and our role to block you: thus turn the wheels of history." They are not saying, "You're behaving disgustingly." It is elusive because American leaders, on the whole, radically and indignantly reject the analysis the French present of U.S. actions. Thus, the French tell the Americans: "We don't want to do or become what you prescribe for us." And the Americans tell the French: "We are not at all what you say we are." France's interpretation of American policy batters America's values, both because it denies the existence of a special, selfless American conscience that distinguishes America from all other previous leading nations, and because it disappoints American expectations of harmony and friendship, especially between old, traditional allies.

Differing Pasts, Positions, and Procedures

In those two patterns of perceptions, or misperceptions, it is easy to see the impact of each nation's past. In the case of France, there is a long tradition of cabinet diplomacy, a long history in which it was often France's turn to be an imperial colossus, a practice of world affairs in which the balance of power is equated with moderation and bipolar alignments are equated with war, a protracted distrust of Anglo-Saxon "sincerity" (exemplified in popular clichés as well as, say, in Michelet), the still considerable pride in having been the first modern state and modern nation, and the more recent experiences of World War II. All of these experiences make for an understandable desire to play a tune of one's own rather than that which someone else has selected, and contribute to the tendency to see in the United States just another dominant power that differs from its predecessors only in its relative greenness and in its capacity for self-delusion. In the case of the United States, the past has not conferred an understanding of and a sympathy for various aspects and practices of European diplomacy, such as the balance of power or self-assertive nationalism. On the other hand, it has conferred a set of values that might be called missionary: the belief that involvement in world affairs in general, and the resort to force and the various wiles and black arts of world politics in particular, can only be justified—and indeed are made imperative—by the need to save the world from chaos and evil, and to establish a pluralistic and progressive order that corresponds to the highest, i.e., non-selfish, interests of all. Moreover, America's past—long periods of isolation broken by briefer periods of involvement either alone or as the dominant power of a coalition—has not prepared the missionary for the frustrating task of cooperating with others as equals. In a nation that has been called "the applied Enlightenment," the expectation of harmony, the faith in consensus among friends breeds an anticipation of compliant collaboration by weaker partners, harnessed to their major ally by a common ideal. America's past leads to diplomatic shortcuts, ellipses, and illusions.

The impact of the two nations' positions on the chessboard of world politics is also important. The United States perceives international affairs, and the behavior of France, from the viewpoint of the superpower that fights an essentially defensive battle in a revolutionary international system. Such a nation tends almost of necessity to appreciate the moves of others in the light of the global strategy that it alone has the responsibility and the means to define and apply. Consequently, the U.S. reacts with less impatience and irritation to limited disagreements within its "camp" and to local challenges from restive associates than to a *défi* as broad and fundamental as de Gaulle's. Narrow dissents affect only the execution of a strategy whose overall design is not attacked; they are minor disturbances within a centrally controlled system. De Gaulle's policy seems to question the very legitimacy of America's postulates, pretenses, and uses of power. It is not surprising that American reactions remind one at times of the shocked and angry responses of a colonial power when rebels ask for independence (ranging from, "Aren't they ungrateful after all we've done for them?" to "We must reassert our leadership and teach them a lesson in power," to "They don't realize that by themselves they couldn't do a thing"). At times, American responses are like the reactions of people established in power and faced not with an equally established opposition, but with a revolutionary one that willfully defies the smooth, orderly procedures of channeled disagreement and denounces as hypocritical the rulers' invocation of legality and higher interest.

France's perceptions, on the other hand, are largely dictated by her position in the postwar world. It is the position of a Western power that needs and accepts America's military protection and at the same time has problems that cannot fail to breed tensions with the United States. For the position of a nation has to be appreciated not merely in abstract terms— prestige, rank in the hierarchy, etc.—but also concretely, in space, and on the time scale. France is a power especially concerned with the German problem and inevitably worried about any policy that would tend to produce complete equality between her and Germany. France is also a power that has suffered enormous losses from the "political collapse" of Europe and of empire; she is inevitably worried about any policy that would tend to perpetuate the partition and divided dependence of Europe, and to dismiss as anachronistic France's residual pretensions as a world power. If America's position is that of the global defensive, France's is that of a global revisionist. For the very existence of Britain as a kind of favored American ally makes it impossible for France to play the smooth (and not very successful) role Britain has tried to play in an effort to return to high rank through cooperating with rather than defying the U.S.

Misperceptions were thus bound to occur. The U.S. could not appreciate, far less sympathize with, a revisionism that appears to us as obsolete and parochial, given our elevated vantage point. From their point of view, however, the French could not fail to see an American strategy that left no room for such revisionism as an obstacle. Having to decide whether it was a deliberate obstacle or an accidental one, they chose the first interpretation because they could not believe that a power in America's position would *not* have a deliberate and consistent policy. Each one, given his position, has been led to a different interpretation of the uses and prospects of power in the nuclear age. The U.S., with the biggest stock of material power in the world, tends to minimize or ignore the very special difficulties that nations face today in translating such a supply into efficient uses, and dismisses as illusory the claims of weaker nations, with comparatively tiny supplies, to an active role. Such claims are seen as puffed up, and such nations are deemed capable of merely "verbal" policies and gestures: they can gesticulate; only the big powers can act. France has a tiny supply and

—for complex reasons in which her past, her position, and American policy figure prominently— little present desire, hope, or possibility of adding the supply of her Western European partners to her own within an integrated community. She therefore finds herself incited to exploit to the hilt the opportunities that the present international system affords to weaker states that are well endowed with all the intangible elements of power, which are so much more evenly distributed than the material assets and so much more exploitable when those assets become at least partly paralyzed or unusable. Since, inevitably, the superpower tries to apply what it has in abundance—military and economic resources—the French tend both to analyze its acts as a deliberate exercise in power politics, and to rejoice at the frequent fiascoes or setbacks that this exercise encounters. A vicious circle sets in: Americans chalk up the "failures" of de Gaulle, thus failing to perceive that the game he plays, with the means he has, is one whose results cannot be assessed in the short run; the French chalk up American failures and attribute them to a kind of *hubris* of power, without taking into account either the way in which Americans, in their own eyes, justify their uses of power, or their attempt to keep those uses restrained, or the fact that the present international system impartially frustrates the designs of the mighty and the not so mighty alike.

Finally, the procedures the two nations follow in their foreign policy account for a considerable part of the differences in their perceptions. American decision-making techniques, which combine a national bent toward *ad hoc* pragmatism and a formidably complex process of intra-agency bargaining and bureaucratic consensus-formation, often result in a series of short-term decisions. The long range is dimly seen, perceived more in the form of general principles of a moral nature, of ideal norms, than as a set of possible and desirable power relations and political connections. Both the magnitude of the tasks undertaken by American foreign-policy-makers and the nature of the machinery tend to produce crisis diplomacy—to yield decisions in and for emergencies, and to leave those decisions intact (or to let their effects run their course) until the next emergency. Hence a general impression of rigidity. For such an approach, France's diplomatic practices are doubly obnoxious. First, the intellectual *démarche* of a man like de Gaulle, moved by a long-range vision of a fundamentally political (rather than moral) nature, strikes policy-makers engaged in the harrowing task of holding the line and coping with trouble all over the globe as presumptuous and irrelevant. Second, the baffling flexibility of French tactics —which display the art of simultaneously pursuing courses that converge in the long run yet conflict in the short run, of leaving options open without avoiding essential choices or losing sight of final goals, and of seizing the best moment for exploiting ambiguous trends—clashes with the habits and expectations of American diplomats. French strategic maneuvers and America's often laborious tactics are in each other's way. On the French side, the custom of starting with a long-range vision or at least with political guidelines is so strong that other nations are always judged as if they too acted in such a fashion. American moves are therefore seen not as improvisations but as the unfolding of a design.

Neither American diplomacy nor Gaullist diplomacy would get very high marks for the ability to cooperate with other nations as equals, to negotiate and to consult with skill and tact. But this common failing breeds different results. On the American side there exists almost a mythology of negotiation, consultation, and cooperation: the methods used for domestic consensus-building are often projected outside, without sufficient awareness of the fact that techniques which work well among domestic partners united on fundamentals are quite incapable, in and of themselves, of producing agreement with foreign partners moved by very different calculations and expectations. What our associates experience as just a routine system of inter-Allied information that does not in the least affect America's monopoly on ultimate decisions, we celebrate as a genuine effort at sharing responsibilities. Consequently, we dismiss French charges about American domination in the diplomacy and strategy of the Alliance as self-serving slurs, and consider French unilateral moves made without consultation as scandalous. We experience their *faits accomplis* as acts of nihilistic defiance, not as reactions to a *status quo* that is disadvantageous to them. As for the French, they interpret the contrast between our words (i.e., our ritual of harmony) and our deeds (i.e., our refusal to share supreme power, as exemplified by the edifying story of our reactions to de Gaulle's famous memorandum of September 1958) both as evidence of a genuine determination to preserve our hegemony and as a license for them to retaliate in kind.

III

The two areas in which French and American perceptions clash most vividly today are Europe and Vietnam.

In Europe American policy-makers appear hesitant, vacillating between two approaches. One is that of the old "situations of strength" policy: the first duty of the West is to organize its own camp, rather than engaging the chief adversary in discussions that will be either divisive or fruitless as long as the Western house has not been put in order. The more recent idea of an Atlantic partnership is a variation on this old design. The other approach, represented by Zbigniew Brzezinski, is that of a deliberate and coordinated "opening to the East" designed to take advantage both of changes in Soviet policy—the shift from total hostility to a more "mixed strategy"—and of the growing desire in both halves of Europe for closer ties across the iron curtain. Both approaches share one dogma: the need for American leadership and Western cohesion. In one version, only such leadership and cohesion can provide Western Europe with military security and exorcise "atavistic" intra-European rivalries; in the other version, only such leadership and cohesion can, in the long run, succeed in shaking off Soviet hegemony in Eastern Europe. In both cases, the dogma has one essential function: to put West Germany into a framework that will give an outlet to her energies and erect a barrier to any eventual "separatism" on her part. From both perspectives, recent French actions are perceived as foolish: from the first, because they jeopardize European security by giving comfort to the Soviets, by complicating Allied communications, and by obliging the Allies to rely more heavily on a nuclear deterrent whose plausibility has decreased in the age of the nuclear stalemate; from the second, because France by herself cannot promote an "opening to the East" that would be favorable to all Western interests. In both cases French moves are seen as giving West Germany a bad example, that of a "*Realpolitik*" which deliberately discards alliance mechanisms and tries to enhance national prestige by direct dealings with Moscow. Thus American officials dislike French moves partly because they are "unreal," and partly because they are only too real, i.e., capable of imitation.

However, the French see in Atlantic "monolithism" the main cause of division and immobility in Europe. They believe that West European security is sufficiently assured by the nuclear stalemate and not significantly enhanced by conventional forces. They deny that a Western bloc led by the U.S. could ever convince the Soviets to consent to German reunification, especially since West German influence would be so strong as to rule out the military and border concessions to Germany's eastern neighbors that would have to be the prerequisites to any reunification. In any event, the French feel that America's drive for an entente with Russia would preclude any great Western effort to change the *status quo* in Europe. Nor do the French believe that West Germany could follow their example and, say, repeat Rapallo: a West Germany detached from and angry at the West would still be potentially so dangerous that the Soviets would hardly be tempted to woo her by giving her East Germany. Thus, to the French, their own design is the only sensible one. They perceive it as a design capable in the long run both of appealing to East Europeans tired of Soviet domination and of getting the Soviets to consent to German re-unification in a framework in which Germany would be, so to speak, contained by European partners East and West, yet no longer tied to the main adversary of the Soviets, whose own military disengagement from the continent would be justified and matched by that of the Americans. American hostility or skepticism toward this design is dismissed as the natural reaction of the monopolist who, deep down, wants to preserve the *status quo*, and whose obstinacy feeds the symmetrical obstinacy of the Soviets. And yet, given the evolution in Western and Eastern Europe and the centrifugal pull of extra-European problems on the U.S. (balance of payments, Vietnam)—an evolution and a pull that both provoke some American disengagement from Europe and prevent a Soviet-American deal to consolidate the *status quo* in Europe—the French feel that they are on the side of "reality." They believe that American policy fights a losing rear-guard battle against those new realities—indeed, a battle against some of its own new inclinations.

In Europe the Franco-American conflict is one of "grand designs," of conceptions of the future, with each antagonist accusing the other of representing the past. To our officials de Gaulle is a relic of cabinet diplomacy. To French officials American policy in one of its approaches is a perpetuation, and in its other a residue of the cold war, of the bipolar world, which new forces and trends have doomed. But the conflict over Vietnam is in a way more pathetic, because it is so retrospective on both sides. Each interprets the Vietnamese situation in the light of its own recent past, projecting on a complex local reality the oversimplifying lessons it feels it has learned recently. The United States got engaged step by step, in a series of *ad hoc*, incremental decisions whose tactical nature conflicts with, gets transfigured into, and is to some extent compensated for by the sweeping general principles that serve to rationalize American intervention in terms familiar to all and appealing to most: resistance to aggression, protection of national independence and of the right to self-determination, containment of Communism, repudiation of Munich. Thus, as the United States sees itself, it is exercising in Vietnam the sad prerogative of leadership and world responsibility; it is repeating the achievements of containment in Europe and Korea in circumstances that are more tragic and confusing; it is applying to China the lessons of twenty years of anti-Communist warfare—limited in its means and objectives yet uncompromising in its principles and scope. Moreover, the procedures used—a combination of overwhelming yet restrained military might and calls for unconditional negotiations

—are those that Americans have habitually applied and that most of them consider balanced and fair.

The French, on the other hand, read the story quite differently. Fifteen years ago they saw themselves as fighting for the West against Asian Communism, and as deserving full support from the United States; but then it was the U.S. that tended to see the French stand as corrupted by colonialism, and to charge the French with throwing local nationalists into the arms of the Communists. Today, the shoe is on the other foot. American officials sound like French Premiers of the early 1950's, while French officials, journalists, and intellectuals describe American policy as if Vietnam were Algeria all over again, and even worse. They point out that at least the French were not aliens in Algeria, whereas the Americans are a foreign interventionist power in Southeast Asia. De Gaulle's Pnompenh speech analyzed America's predicament in "Algerian" terms: (1) it is an internal war (between natives and a Western power), not a case of aggression; (2) force alone offers no way out, for the heart of the matter lies in the Western power's inability to find an organized native political force capable of depriving the rebellion of its cause, cadres, and control; (3) in such a war the myth and mystique of "unconditional negotiations" are of little avail, for the rebel force will not engage in formal talks until the Western power has outlined in acceptable detail its proposals about the political future of the disputed land; (4) no real prestige is lost by an honest confession of error and an intelligent effort at disengagement.

Two completely conflicting analyses lead to a mountain of misunderstandings and a morass of mutual recriminations. American defenders of official policy feel deeply hurt by the French analysis. They detect in it traces of *Schadenfreude*, an indecent French desire for Americans to fail where France has failed, a kind of delayed wish for revenge. (But they do not notice that many of their bitterest French critics were also in the vanguard of opposition to French colonialism.) Even if they did notice it, Americans would not feel less hurt, for any comparison between a colonial situation and their role in Vietnam—between a Communist-led national revolution against imperialism and what they see as Communist imperialism attacking a free nation—is an insult. Moreover, France's position is resented both because it encourages the enemy and because France's advice comes cheap, her present responsibilities being as small as her past responsibility looms large. The French, for their part, dismiss as insignificant or illusory the differences between Vietnam and colonial wars. They choose to see as the only reality the use of force by the most powerful white nation against a small yellow people for the preservation of a power position threatened by local revolutionary discontent. American denials are denounced as either hypocritical or obtuse, and once more the French point to the contradiction between professions of faith or intent and daily acts. The very fact that here (by contrast with Europe) French views are deprived of immediate potency deepens the rift: for while they increase American resentment, they give good conscience to the French, who are moved to heights of self-righteous and indignant lucidity now that their own record has been swept clean by decolonization, and convinced that their very disinterestedness ought to make American officialdom pay special attention to their analysis.

Ultimately, "reality" will be determined not only by those deep trends with which both sides profess to be aligned, and which are still ambiguous, but also by the acts of statesmen aimed at shaping those trends in a definite way. To decide here and now who appears to be the better analyst and the better manipulator would require another essay. All I wanted to suggest is that alongside Machiavelli or Rousseau, Pirandello ought to have his place in the pantheon of international-relations theory.

JOHN G. STOESSINGER

China and America: The Burden
of Past Misperceptions

History, in psychological terms, is the memory of nations. It is the reposi-
tory not only of objective events but also of illusions and misunderstandings that filter down to our own time. Many Americans are profoundly
anxious about the course of Chinese-American relations, but far too few
of us are aware of the psychological roots of the present encounter. These
roots go deep and are grounded in a soil of misperceptions that have marred
relations between China and America since the very beginning. Perhaps an
analysis of this tragic past may better equip us to deal with the even more
tragic present.

I

The First Encounter

Ours is the first century in over two thousand years in which China has
not considered herself to be at the center of the universe. For two millennia
the Chinese Empire conceived of itself as the hub of civilization, the great
school of the world—much as Athens had once considered itself to be
the school of the ancient Mediterranean world. Although dynasties came

John G. Stoessinger is the Executive Officer of the doctoral program in political science
at the City University of New York and a visiting professor of international relations at
Columbia University, where he lectures to the International Fellows Program. His book,
The Might of Nations, won the Bancroft Prize in 1962. His other books include *The
Refugee and the World Community, Organizing Peace in the Nuclear Age, Financing
the United Nations System,* and *The United Nations and the Superpowers.*

and went, the political structure of the Empire remained essentially stable. The Emperor, aided by a small intellectual elite, controlled the government. He ruled by the Mandate of Heaven, and his edicts had the authority of a philosopher-king. His vast realm, which stretched from Siberia to the tropics, was known as "all under heaven."

The world beyond the Great Wall of China did not hold much interest since, in the eyes of the Chinese, it was populated by barbarians. Hence the foreign relations of the Empire for two thousand years were essentially tributary relationships: long caravans laden with gifts for the Emperor would weave their way across the land to the Imperial Court at Peking; the envoy would kowtow before the Son of Heaven and present the tribute. The act of kowtow left no doubt in anyone's mind as to who was superior and who inferior in status. It consisted of three separate kneelings, each kneeling accompanied by three separate prostrations, all performed to the command of a court usher: "Kneel!" "Fall prostrate!" "Rise to your knees!" All envoys went through these calisthenics, and their proper performance was merely regarded as good manners by the Emperor and his entourage. The Chinese believed that it was perfectly self-evident that their Empire was a superior civilization, and the act of kowtow was a symbolic recognition of this axiomatic truth.

This Chinese view of themselves made them a stay-at-home people. Since the Empire contained everything of value, no one wanted to go abroad and thus be exiled from civilization. There was no interest in the conquest of strange lands of lesser value. An "Office for Barbarian Affairs" was in charge of all foreign, that is, tributary, relations. On reading the descriptions of "Western barbarians" one is struck with a fuzzy-minded, fairy-story quality not unlike that which characterized the descriptions of Western travelers to "Cathay." The barbarians were thought to inhabit small islands separated from civilization by "intervening wastes of sea." They were described as having skins of "dazzling white color," beaked noses, and flaming red hair. No distinction was made among the multifarious "tribes" of barbarians. In all cases the Chinese attitude was a mixture of indifference and contempt.

The first attempt by a Westerner to pierce this curtain of ignorance took place in the sixteenth century, when a Jesuit priest, Matthew Ricci, set out to convert China to Catholicism. Marco Polo's travels to China in the twelfth century had had a significant impact on Europe but almost none on China. Ricci arrived in China in 1583, at the time of the Catholic Counter Reformation, and engaged in a thirty-year effort to convert China from the top. This resourceful Jesuit mastered the Chinese language, dressed in the garb of a Confucian literatus, and adapted himself to the customs of the land. His knowledge of mathematics and astronomy earned him the respect of Chinese scholars and even got him an audience with the Emperor. As he saw it, his first mission was to show the Chinese that their view of the world was false:

> Their universe was limited to their own fifteen provinces, and in the sea painted around it they had placed a few little islands to which they gave the names of different kingdoms they had heard of. All of these islands put together would not be as large as the smallest of the Chinese provinces. With such a limited knowledge, it is evident why they boasted of their kingdom as being the whole world, and why they called it Thienhia, meaning, everything under the heavens. When they learned that China was only a part of the great east, they considered such an idea, so unlike their own, to be something utterly impossible . . . .[1]

Ricci's educational effort aroused such resistance and even fury that the Jesuit had to settle for a tactful compromise. Although he did include the Western empires on a map that he had prepared, giving them Chinese names in the process, he kept China in the central position.

> They could not comprehend the demonstrations proving that the earth is a globe, made up of land and water, and that a globe by its very nature has neither beginning nor end. The geographer was therefore obliged to change his design and, by omitting the first meridian, he left a margin on either side of the map, making the Kingdom of China appear right in the center. This was more in keeping with their ideas and it gave them a great deal of pleasure and satisfaction.[2]

When Matthew Ricci died in China in 1610, his famous map did not long survive him. It had made a sufficient impact, however, to fix in the minds of the ruling Chinese Confucian scholars the names of the great Western empires, although their exact location was soon forgotten. During the next two centuries, right up to the time of the Opium War, total confusion dominated Chinese perceptions of the outside world. Contemporary maps show islands named France, Spain, Portugal, England, Italy, and America, rotating like satellites around the great sun of the Celestial Empire. Their location often bore little resemblance to reality. Ricci had briefly lifted the veil; but very soon after his death it descended again, and the "barbarians"

---

[1] *China in the Sixteenth Century; The Journals of Matthew Ricci, 1583-1610*, trans. by Louis J. Gallagher, S. J. (New York: Random House, 1953), p. 166.
[2] *Ibid.*, p. 167.

were relegated once more to obscurity. Only vague memories of strange names connoting quaint and faraway places remained.[3]

When in 1793, Lord Macartney, the leader of a trade mission from Great Britain, refused to perform the kowtow upon his arrival in Peking, he was refused an audience with the Emperor, who sent the following rebuff to King George:

> You, O King, are so inclined toward our civilization that you have sent a special envoy across the seas to bring to our Court your memorial of congratulations on the occasion of my birthday and to present your native products as an expression of your thoughtfulness.
> . . . . The various articles presented by you, O King, this time are accepted by my special order to the office in charge of such functions in consideration of the offerings having come from a long distance with sincere good wishes. As a matter of fact, the virtue and prestige of the Celestial Dynasty having spread far and wide, the kings of myriad nations come by land and sea with all sorts of precious things. Consequently there is nothing we lack, as your principal envoy and others have themselves observed. We have never set much store on strange or ingenious objects, nor do we need any more of your country's manufactures . . . . [4]

The American Revolution, which occurred toward the end of Emperor Ch'ien Lung's reign, must have seemed to him like an insignificant squabble between white barbarians somewhere in the outer darkness. Perhaps he never even heard of it. At any rate when the first American ship, the *Empress of China*, reached Canton in 1784 "in the adventurous pursuit of commerce," her master, Captain John Green, was received as just another "white barbarian," although he managed to sell his cargo of furs, cotton, and ginseng weed—which Chinese officials believed would restore their virility—for an enormous profit. By 1789, the year George Washington was inaugurated as President, fifteen American vessels were carrying on trade with China.

The first serious controversy involving Americans and Chinese starkly demonstrated the Chinese attitude. In 1821, a Chinese woman who was peddling fruit alongside the ship *Emily*, which was anchored in Canton, fell into the water and drowned. Captain Howland of the *Emily* claimed that the death was an accident, but the Chinese officials at Canton insisted

[3] John K. Fairbank, *Trade and Diplomacy on the China Coast*, Vol. I (Cambridge: Harvard University Press, 1953), p. 10.
[4] Quoted in *China's Response to the West: A Documentary Survey*, ed. by John K. Fairbank and Ssu-yu Teng (Cambridge: Harvard University Press, 1954), p. 19.

that an American sailor, one Francis Terranova, had caused the woman's death by hurling a heavy object at her. They now demanded a life for a life, insisting that the sailor be handed over or else all trade with the Americans would be stopped immediately. The Americans, in a quandary, refused to hand over Terranova, but permitted the Chinese to try him on a murder charge aboard the *Emily*. The Chinese found him guilty and sentenced him to death by strangulation. The Americans reluctantly complied with a demand for his surrender, and Terranova was executed by the local Cantonese authorities. Shortly after the sentence was carried out, an imperial edict reached the Americans that permitted them to continue their trading; but it left no doubt in their minds about the Emperor's view of them. "As the dispositions of these foreigners are depraved by the education and customs of countries beyond the bounds of civilization," the edict read, "they are incapable of following right reason; their characters are deformed; their perverse obstinacy is untameable; and they are dead to the influence of our renovating laws and manners."[5] The Son of Heaven was so moved to compassion, however, by a people so dependent upon the products of the Celestial Dynasty that he was willing to permit them to continue their tribute-bearing activities.

These conditions prevailed until the year 1839, when the flourishing opium traffic off the China coast precipitated a major crisis between Britain and China. In the autumn of that year the Chinese Emperor was so disturbed about the ravages of the drug upon his people that he sent a stern protest to Queen Victoria:

> We find that your country is sixty or seventy thousand li [three li make one mile, ordinarily] from China. Yet there are barbarian ships that strive to come here for trade for the purpose of making a profit. I have heard that the smoking of opium is very strictly forbidden by your country; that is because the harm caused by opium is clearly understood. Let us ask, where is your conscience?[6]

The Emperor concluded with the statement that the "barbarians" could not get along for a single day without two major Chinese exports, tea and rhubarb, and threatened Queen Victoria with an embargo: "If China cuts off these benefits with no sympathy for those who are to suffer, then what can the barbarians rely upon to keep themselves alive?"

The protest went unheeded, and finally the Emperor appointed one of

[5] Foster Rhea Dulles, *China and America* (Princeton: Princeton University Press, 1946), p. 13.
[6] *China's Response to the West*, p. 25.

his officials, Commissioner Lin, to blockade British merchants at Canton and to destroy their opium. The British interpreted this seizure as an interference with freedom of trade and as an act of aggression. Instead of ending the smuggling of opium, Commissioner Lin had precipitated the Opium War. The war was little more than a skirmish, during which the British destroyed the Chinese forts at Canton and imposed upon the Empire the Treaty of Nanking of 1842. The Opium War, which was the first violent encounter between China and a Western nation, came as a terrible shock to the Chinese. It was as if the world had suddenly been turned upside down. Strange and inferior peoples known to them only through folklore and myth had suddenly assaulted them out of nowhere and broken their ramparts with superior firepower. As one Chinese edict submitted to the British shortly before the signing of the Treaty of Nanking put it: "Except for your ships being solid, your gunfire fierce, and your rockets powerful, what other abilities have you?"[7]

The Treaty of Nanking compelled the Imperial Government to open not only Canton but four other ports—Amoy, Ningpo, Foochow, and Shanghai—to British trade. Moreover, Britain exacted from China a heavy indemnity and the cession of the island of Hong Kong. At the time the Treaty was being signed, an American sea captain, Commodore Lawrence Kearney of the *Constellation*, was in Canton. The captain sized up the situation and immediately demanded from Commissioner Ch'i-Ying, the Chinese negotiator, that "the trade and commerce of the United States be placed upon the same footing as the nation most favored."[8] This demand was granted, and shortly thereafter the first United States minister to the Chinese Empire, Caleb Cushing, a lawyer from Newburyport, Massachusetts, arrived in Canton with a naval squadron of four vessels in order to formalize this agreement. The first Chinese-American treaty, which granted the United States privileges equal to those exacted by Britain, was signed at Wanghia in July 1844.

The Chinese negotiators were simply defenseless in the face of Western guns. But they also deeply believed in their own cultural superiority and in the "backwardness" of the white barbarians in everything but firepower. Ch'i-Ying, before sitting down with the British and Americans, made it his business to study these strange tribes. A short excerpt from his observations is revealing:

> As to these various countries, although they have rulers, they may be
> either male or female, and they may rule variously for a long or short

[7] *Ibid.*, p. 36.
[8] Dulles, *op. cit.*, p. 28.

time, all of which is far beyond the bounds of any system of laws. For example, the English barbarians are ruled by a female, the Americans and the French are ruled by males, the English and French rulers both rule for life, while the ruler of the American barbarians is established by the campaigning of his countrymen, and is changed once in four years—after he leaves the position, he is of equal rank with the common people.[9]

Ch'i-Ying hoped that exposing the barbarians for a short period of time to China's superior civilization would cause them to recognize their own inferiority and humble them into withdrawing. Hence, the correct way of dealing with the barbarians was to conciliate them and to play them off against each other. For example, Ch'i-Ying thought nothing of giving the Americans the right to try their own citizens who committed crimes on Chinese soil. In his view, an arrangement whereby the barbarians would administer justice to their own nationals and assume responsibility for their good behavior could only be of advantage to the Imperial Government. Upon concluding the Treaty of Wanghia with Ambassador Cushing, Ch'i-Ying stated that "he could not restrain his spirit from delight and his heart from dilating with joy."[10] This was the beginning of American extraterritorial rights in China.

* * * *

Early American images of China were deeply colored by the Marco Polo story. At the time the *Empress of China* sailed into Canton harbor, "Cathay" was described as a great, ancient, and exotic culture devoted to the arts and sciences. The founders of the American Republic knew that the Chinese had invented such things as paper, gunpowder, and the compass, and that they had great sages and philosophers. Symbolic of this period was the American conception of Confucius as a venerable Chinese sage who had developed a profound ethical system centuries before the West had become civilized. Actually Confucius had been a contemporary of Plato. It is interesting to note that aspects of this "Marco Polo image" of China have survived down to our own day. For example, in 1956 a TV "spectacular" on Marco Polo made the point that the hero spent an entire year in the study of philosophy in order to prepare himself for his trip. At the end of the year he stated that he had now acquired the knowledge normally possessed in China by any nine-year-old boy.[11]

[9] *China's Response to the West*, p. 39.
[10] Dulles, *op. cit.*, p. 29.
[11] Harold R. Isaacs, *Images of Asia* (New York: Capricorn Books, 1962), p. 90.

Once the seafaring Yankees of the Canton trade had established actual physical contact, American images of China changed drastically. Most of the Americans who came to China in these early days were interested either in making a profit or in making converts or in both. Both merchants and missionaries soon began to view China as a "backward" nation. The exotic and the odd about the Chinese now acquired a tinge of the inferior. In almost all of the travelogues of this period there are stories about pigtails, bound feet, ancestor worship, female infanticide, and a host of other sinister practices. Life in China was no longer described as superior but as upside down: the people read from right to left, wrote their surnames ahead of their given names, served soup as the last course of a meal, made a gesture for "come here" when they meant "goodbye." The once-respected Chinese became "Chinamen;" the bearers of a superior civilization became "teeming faceless millions;" and the originators of a profound ethical system became "godless heathens." The superior attitude of Chinese officials toward Americans was perceived as grotesque arrogance. In Harold Isaac's telling phrase, the Age of Respect was giving way to the Age of Contempt.

The American reaction to the Terranova incident was already symptomatic of this transition. The murder trial was described as a farce, and only the lack of effective protection by their own government, fear of losing their lucrative trade, and their helpless position in Canton made the Americans surrender Terranova to the Cantonese officials. However, the *Emily's* captain expressed the bitter feelings of the Americans in the following note to the Chinese Government:

> We are bound to submit to your laws while we are in your waters, be they ever so unjust. You have, following your ideas of justice, condemned the man unheard. You have the power to compel us. We believe the man innocent; when he is taken from the ship, the commander strikes his colors.[12]

Twenty years later the Americans had reversed the balance of power.

By the time Ambassador Cushing sailed into Canton in the shadow of British gunboats, the Americans' conception of China was practically a mirror image of that of the latter. Cushing was to take no presents to the Emperor in order that they would not be misinterpreted as tribute. Instead, a varied collection of scientific objects was assembled to impress the Chinese with the technological achievements of the United States. A list of these objects is worth mentioning: a pair of six-shooters, models of a steam

[12] Dulles, *op. cit.*, p. 15.

excavator and a steam vessel, a daguerreotype apparatus, a telescope, a barometer, and the Encyclopedia Americana. Cushing bore a letter of introduction from President Tyler that addressed the Son of Heaven in a tone customarily reserved for petty American Indian chiefs:

> Great and Good Friend: I hope your health is good. China is a great empire, extending over a great part of the world. The Chinese are numerous. You have millions and millions of subjects. The twenty-six United States are as large as China. Our territories extend from one great ocean to the other . . . .

> I therefore send to your Court Caleb Cushing, one of the wise and learned men of this country. On his first arrival in China, he will inquire for your health. He has then strict orders to go to your great city of Pekin, and there to deliver this letter . . . .[13]

Cushing's mission, as we have seen, was a great success. The Americans secured the most-favored-nation privileges they had come to get, including extraterritorial rights. Although these rights were initially granted by the Chinese in the hope of persuading the foreigners to withdraw after they realized their own inferiority, the Americans interpreted the Chinese concessions as appeasement stemming from weakness. They had come to force the Chinese to treat them as equals. In the process, American perceptions of China changed so greatly that the scales were completely reversed. It was now the Chinese who were treated as inferior. This first encounter between China and America was thus a surprise to both sides: to the Chinese because they found themselves unable to eject the "barbarians" through moral suasion; and to the Americans because they encountered almost no effective military resistance.

* * * *

The most striking thing about the early images China and America held of one another was how little resemblance they bore to reality. This is not too surprising since nothing in the past of these two nations prepared them for the violent encounter to follow. Matthew Ricci's effort to teach the Chinese about the outside world was only a ripple on a sea of illusions that had remained placid for thousands of years. When Caleb Cushing's naval squadron entered Canton harbor, Confucian scholars had to learn about America like children in school. The first Chinese researcher on the United

States, Hsu Chi-yu, wrote a primer in 1848 with the following description of Washington:

> There was a certain Wa-sheng-tun [Washington] born in 1731 [sic]. When he was ten he lost his father, and his mother educated him and brought him up. He had cherished great ambitions in youth and was gifted in both literary and military matters. When the time came for the multitude of the people to revolt against the British, they urged Tun [Washington] to be their commander . . . .[14]

The Americans, on their part, brimming with ideas of innovation and revolution, quickly lost respect for a civilization that placed little value on expansion and technical progress. Admiration for a superior culture quickly changed after actual contact to disdain for a "backward" people. Americans had little patience with a static bureaucracy that could not even defend itself.

Almost everything about the two societies was different. Ancient China venerated tradition above all else. All inspiration came from the past, and history was the queen of the sciences. Early America, on the other hand, looked to the future. Age was a liability, not an asset. The earth's resources had to be harnessed, and its frontiers had to be explored rather than ignored.

What finally brought the two societies into contact with one another was the coming of the new imperial age of the nineteenth century, which helped unleash the expansionary drives of America. The two nations met in the crucible of a revolutionary world in which one regarded itself as the bearer of tradition and the other became associated with its destruction. The expansion of Europe that created America also destroyed the old China. China made her stand against this modern world, stunned and bewildered. America had helped to invent it.

It is reasonable to assume that had the West not forced open the Chinese door, China's image of herself and of the West would have continued undisturbed. But given the dynamism of Western expansion, the meeting between China and America was probably inevitable. What made it into a tragedy, however, were the illusions that the main actors harbored about one another. The Chinese self-image left no room for learning from the outside world; barbarians would always remain barbarians. The early Americans, on the other hand, held directly opposite views; they went to slay dragons in a land where the dragon stood for almost everything that was good. And thus this first encounter, marked by misperceptions on both sides, became the seedbed for the great conflicts to follow.

[14] *China's Response to the West*, p. 44.

II

The Boxer Uprising And The Open Door

The story of China's dismemberment at the hands of the Western powers in the nineteenth century has often been told. Yet most Western accounts do not fully grasp the fact that this event was probably the greatest disaster that befell China in her entire history. A civilization that saw itself at the top was brought low by the gunboats of a group of assorted "barbarians." After the Opium War, a scramble for concessions in China took place that had reduced China's sovereignty to little more than a fiction. By 1900 the British, the French, and the Japanese had all defeated China and exacted territorial concessions and spheres of influence. The Russians and Germans had also secured extraterritorial rights, with the result that in most of China's coastal cities, as well as in the capital of Peking, foreign laws reigned supreme and Chinese were treated as inferiors in their own country. This writer still recalls how, upon arriving in Shanghai in 1941, he was shocked to see a sign affixed to a foreign country club in the international settlement that read: "Dogs and Chinese not permitted." The United States fought no colonial wars in China, but benefited from all the concessions exacted by the other Western powers. Although the British had brought the first gunboats into the harbor of Canton, Caleb Cushing of the United States had brought his naval squadron, too. And in 1858, while British and French gunboats besieged Tientsin, an American minister waited some distance up the river and then joined with the other envoys in signing a treaty securing America's share of Chinese territory.

What reduced the old China to dust was, of course, the superior fire-power of foreign cannon. But if we are to understand the Chinese reaction at a deeper level we must ask why they were so slow to respond. The answer may be found in the Chinese images of themselves and of the West, particularly on the matter of physical force.

Throughout the entire history of the Chinese Empire, the ultimate sanction of rule was the virtuous conduct of the Son of Heaven, which was thought to inspire respect, obedience, and loyalty. In all their foreign relations the Chinese kept this myth intact, even when they were weak. When 3,000 Mongol horsemen threatened Peking, they were given lavish gifts by the Emperor; but he insisted that their visit be called a tribute mission. Thus, the fiction of superiority was maintained, and since the recorded "facts" substantiated the theory, it became self-perpetuating. Physical force simply seemed unimportant in this context.

Hence, when five major Western powers intruded into China, the one thing that could have stopped the assault was lacking in the Chinese attitude: the resolution to meet force with force. Instead, old techniques were applied to the new situation. The "barbarians" were conciliated or played off against each other, usually with disastrous results. The Chinese army was decades behind its Western counterparts. It was simply a rabble provided with bags of rice and an assortment of antiquated weapons, including umbrellas, fans, gaily colored flags, and heavy swords. Men of good family would not join the army since it was known everywhere that Confucius had held that "good iron is not used for nails and good men are not used for soldiery."

Until the scramble for concessions threatened to swallow up China altogether, the Kuang-hsü Emperor was complacent in his conviction that the time-honored techniques would work. Among the few men who perceived reality more accurately was K'ang Yu-wei, a reformer who appealed to the Emperor in 1895 urging a thoroughgoing overhaul of the Empire if the situation was to be saved. His memorial is a poignant document:

> If Your Majesty will not decide, or will prefer to remain in the old grooves of the Conservatives, then your territories will be swallowed up, your limbs will be bound, your viscera will be cut up, and Your Majesty will scarcely manage to retain your throne or to rule over more than a fragment of your ancient Empire.[15]

Unless China modernized and developed firepower to expel the foreign devils, "she would sink in the earth, be buried in ruins, burst like an egg, and be torn to shreds." Finally, in 1898, Kuang-hsü listened and attempted some reforms. But he was no Peter the Great. The resistance of the Confucian conservatives was too strong, and later that year the old Empress Dowager, Tzu Hsi, deposed him in a *coup d'état* and assumed control of the government. The short-lived reforms came to an abrupt end. The old Empress nurtured a fierce hatred for the "foreign devils." In an edict of November 1899, she complained that "the various powers cast upon China looks of tiger-like voracity, hustling each other in their endeavors to be the first to seize upon her innermost territories."[16] Yet she refused to meet the challenge realistically; and when the old China finally did respond with violence, the result was a fiasco.

At about the time of the old Empress' edict, a popular movement flared up in northern China describing itself as the Fists of Righteous Harmony,

[15] Quoted in William L. Langer, *The Diplomacy of Imperialism*, Vol. II (New York: Alfred A. Knopf, 1935), p. 677.
[16] *Ibid.*, p. 693.

to be known later and more popularly as the Boxers. The movement was held together by a fierce hatred of the Westerners, their ceaseless pressure on the homeland, and their interference with indigenous customs. Many of the Boxers believed, for example, that the "foreign devils" had built railroads and telegraph lines for the express purpose of murdering the good spirits of the harvest; for when it rained, the wires would rust and reddish drops would fall to the ground, obviously the blood of good spirits impaled on the wires. The "barbarians" had also built buildings steeper than any ever seen before in China, obviously constructed so that benevolent spirits, flying low over the countryside, would crash into them. Worse, the foreigners had disturbed ancestral burial grounds, desecrated holy places, and turned the Temple of Heaven in Peking into a tourist attraction. By early 1900, armed bands were roaming the countryside burning foreign property and taking the lives of "secondary devils," Chinese converts to Christianity. Peking was soon encircled by fanatical bands, who no longer concealed their object of driving all the barbarians into the sea. The old Empress, herself fiercely xenophobic, gave the movement her tacit and, at times, open support.

The story of the Boxers' siege of Peking is well known and will not be recounted here. What is less well known is the Boxers' image of themselves that led them directly to their disastrous defeat. They believed, in effect, that they were invulnerable, that Western bullets could not harm them since right and justice were on their side. In April 1900, for example, placards appeared all over Peking proclaiming that God himself had come down to earth to support the Boxers in their struggle.

> In a certain street in Peking some worshippers at midnight suddenly saw a spirit descend in their midst. The spirit was silent for a long time. Then a terrible voice was heard saying: I am none other than the Great Yu Ti [God of the unseen world] come down in person. Disturbances are to be dreaded from the foreign devils; everywhere they are erecting telegraphs and building railways. Their sins are numberless as the hair on the head. Therefore am I wroth and my thunders have pealed forth. I have given forth my decree that I shall descend to earth at the head of all the saints and spirits and wherever the I-ho Chuan [Boxers] are gathered together, there shall the Gods be in the midst of them. Therefore I expressly command you to make this known in every place . . . . [17]

Encouraged by their self-proclaimed invulnerability and "800,000 spirit

[17] Quoted in G. N. Steiger, *China and the Occident* (New Haven: Yale University Press, 1927), pp. 144-45.

soldiers," the Boxers burst into Peking in June 1900, assassinated the German and the Japanese ministers, and laid siege to the foreign legations. During the fifty-five days of the siege, the Empress vacillated. One day she would send supplies to the beleaguered legations and, on the next, urge the Boxer leaders to destroy them. At any time, she could have lifted the siege or crushed the foreigners. But she did neither. It is highly probable that her ambivalence stemmed from her old Confucian convictions that violence was to be avoided, on the one hand, and her intense desire to get rid of the barbarians, on the other. At any rate, when the international relief expedition entered Peking and lifted the siege in August, the old Empress fled the capital, leaving the responsibility of dealing with the victorious foreigners to a veteran Chinese diplomat, Li Hung-chang.

After the Boxer fiasco, China could do nothing but agree to the harsh terms imposed upon her by the Western powers. The Boxer Protocol of 1901 included several items bitterly resented by the Imperial Court; however, there was no alternative but to accept them. The leaders of the uprising were to be executed, and monuments to foreigners who had lost their lives were to be erected in each of the foreign settlements. The importation of arms and ammunition was to be prohibited for five years, and an indemnity of 450 million taels was imposed on the Chinese treasury. In the words of one thoughtful student of the period, the function of the Manchu Government now became little more than a debt-collecting agency for the foreign powers.[18] Thus ended the old China's last attempt to free itself of foreign penetration.

* * * *

At the time the Boxer uprising was beginning to smolder in the Chinese countryside, the United States was deeply preoccupied with the Spanish-American War. But after Admiral Dewey's victory and President McKinley's famous decision to annex the Philippines "after having walked the floor of the White House all night," the attention of the United States Government began to shift to the Far East. The quest for concessions by the European powers worried American business interests, who feared that they might be frozen out of China altogether. Pressures for a more spirited Far Eastern policy mounted during 1899 and finally led to the famous American circular letter to the European powers known as the Open Door notes. What is interesting for our purposes is the astounding difference between what most American leaders at the time believed the Open Door to

[18] Chester Tan, *The Boxer Catastrophe* (New York: Columbia University Press, 1955), pp. 215-36.

be and what it really was. Many of these misperceptions have lived down to our own day.

The Open Door notes of September 1899 are usually associated with the American Secretary of State, John Hay. Actually, they were deeply influenced by two other men, one an American, the other a Britisher. When John Hay became Secretary of State in late 1898, he had no adviser on Far Eastern affairs. He himself had never been to China, and he had only a cursory knowledge of the Far East. Thus, he brought with him to Washington an old friend, William W. Rockhill, who had served in the diplomatic corps in China. Rockhill himself, however, had not been to China in seven years and was somewhat out of touch with the rapidly moving events there. In June 1898, a friend of Rockhill's, the Englishman A. E. Hippisley of the Chinese Imperial Customs Service, passed through Washington on his way to England. Hippisley was concerned about the threat posed by other European powers to British commercial interests in China. Britain controlled about eighty per cent of the Western trade with China and wanted to keep it that way.[19] Hence, Hippisley urged Rockhill to persuade Hay to approach the European powers and get from them an assurance that there would be no interference with foreign trade in their respective spheres of influence. Spheres of influence, he said, were here to stay and had to be treated as existing facts.[20] Rockhill sensed a congruence of British and American interests in China. He realized that such an American approach to the European powers would serve a double purpose: it would restate the most-favored-nation principle that the United States had enunciated at the Treaty of Wanghia in 1844, but it would also put the United States on record as being against the further dismemberment of the Chinese Empire. Hay was impressed and, after some initial fears of playing into the hands of Great Britain, decided to go along with Rockhill's recommendation. The result was a circular memorandum dispatched on September 6, 1899, to London, St. Petersburg, and Berlin, and a month later to Paris, Rome, and Tokyo in which the United States asked the six powers concerned not to interfere in each others' treaty ports and spheres of influence and to observe trade equality for everyone. These were the original Open Door notes.

Upon close scrutiny, the notes did not amount to very much. In the first place, they were inspired by a British subject and were in essence a restatement of British policy. Indeed, William Langer asserts that "the

[19] George F. Kennan, *American Diplomacy, 1900-1950* (New York: Mentor Books, 1951), p. 27.
[20] *Ibid.*, p. 34.

American position was exactly that of Britain."[21] Second, they represented no novel departure for the United States, but merely reasserted privileges claimed by and granted to the United States half a century earlier. Third, the replies of the six powers were evasive and noncommittal. The American ambassador at St. Petersburg, for example, warned Hay that the Russian Government "did not wish to answer the propositions at all and finally did so with great reluctance."[22] Nevertheless, Hay announced on March 20, 1900, that he had received "satisfactory assurances from all the powers addressed" and that he regarded each as "final and definitive."[23] Finally, the notes had little if any bearing on the fate of China. They were dispatched only a few months before the Boxer fiasco and its bitter consequences for the Chinese Empire.

The interpretation put upon the Open Door notes by the American public at the time was very different. Almost without exception, the American press hailed the notes as a triumph of American diplomacy. The *Chicago Herald* declared that "there had never been a more brilliant and important achievement in diplomacy," and the *New York Evening Post* described the notes as a "noble work of peace." The two major political parties voiced their approval. The prevailing opinion was well summed up by one contemporary publicist:

> The "open-door" policy in China was an American idea. It was set up in contrast to the "spheres-of-influence" policy practised by other nations . . . .
>
> The "open-door" is one of the most creditable episodes in American diplomacy, an example of benevolent impulse accompanied by energy and shrewd skill in negotiation. Not one of the statesmen and nations that agreed to Hay's policy wanted to. It was like asking every man who believes in truth to stand up—the liars are obliged to be the first to rise. Hay saw through them perfectly; his insight into human nature was one of his strongest qualities.[24]

The gap between reality and the American perception of the Open Door is not difficult to explain. The Hay notes committed the United States to absolutely nothing. There was no sacrifice of any kind. Yet the formula had a lofty and idealistic ring that sounded well at home. It made the United States appear as the arbiter among the self-seeking European powers and

[21] Langer, *op. cit.*, p. 687.
[22] Tyler Dennett, *John Hay* (New York: Macmillan, 1933), p. 294.
[23] A. Whitney Griswold, *The Far Eastern Policy of the United States* (New York: Harcourt, Brace, and Co., 1938), p. 78.
[24] Mark Sullivan, *Our Times: The Turn of the Century* (New York: Macmillan, 1926), p. 509.

the protector of the weak. The very term "Open Door" suggested rights of equal opportunity without fear of favor. And the United States was to be their guarantor.

Actually the Open Door notes were quickly overtaken by events. Three months after Hay noted his satisfaction with the responses of the European powers to his circular memorandum, the Boxers laid siege to Peking. On July 3, 1900, in the midst of the siege, Hay sent a follow-up circular note to the powers in which he reiterated the points made earlier and added that it was "the policy of the Government of the United States to seek to preserve the Chinese territorial and administrative entity." Once again the reaction of the American public was favorable, and the image of the United States as the protector of China permeated the American press. However, as George F. Kennan points out, this second set of notes had no practical effect outside the United States.[25] In fact, by August 1900, the international relief expedition was on its way to Peking. Twenty-five hundred of the 19,000 allied troops were Americans; and the United States was one of the signatories of the Boxer Protocol of 1901.

Although the United States Government was at first hesitant to take an active part in the suppression of the Boxer uprising, the siege of its legation in Peking tipped the scales. The American minister in Peking, E. H. Conger, encouraged legation guards to open fire on Chinese troops and called these actions "exhibitions of skill and courage that would serve as good object lessons."[26] Americans generally regarded the Boxers as ruffians who deserved the same treatment as ordinary criminals. Most contemporary American diplomats tended to regard the Protocol of 1901 as a lenient settlement for China.[27]

The final irony occurred in November 1900, when John Hay, the author of the policy of the Open Door, instructed his minister in Peking to seek a naval base and territorial concession for the United States at Samsah Bay in Fukien province, thus abandoning the basic premise of his entire policy. This American attempt to join in the scramble for concessions was thwarted by the Japanese Government, which politely pointed out that Fukien was within its sphere of influence and noted its surprise that the United States, of all powers, should attempt to interfere. Hay abandoned the venture in disillusionment, and Rockhill, in a letter to Hippisley, expressed the hope that it would be "a long time before the United States

[25] Kennan, *op. cit.*, p. 38.
[26] Steiger, *op. cit.*, pp. 221-22.
[27] Edward Thomas Williams, *China Yesterday and Today* (New York: Thomas Y. Crowell Co., 1923), p. 424.

would get into another muddle of this description."[28] Thus ended the American policy of the Open Door in China.

Conclusions

The misperceptions that plagued the relations between China and America during the latter half of the nineteenth century added enormously to the tragedy of the encounter. Half a century separated Caleb Cushing's arrival in Canton from the Boxer uprising. During that period the leadership of the Chinese Empire did not alter its self-image of moral and cultural superiority and its conviction that the barbarians would recognize this superiority and behave like the tribute-bearing missions of old. Nor did it recognize the Western cannon as a totally new factor to be reckoned with, but rather preferred to meet physical force with the time-honored tactics of conciliation. Even extraterritorial concessions were not resented at first; rather, they were seen as an expedient way of allowing the barbarians to apply their own laws to their fellow barbarians without involving China. There was little if any feeling of Chinese nationalism in those early days.

As the European powers began to carve up China in earnest and the competition for concessions gathered speed, the Imperial Government was forced to acquiesce almost without resistance. Only in 1900, when the capital itself was divided up and the hated barbarians had reached the Temple of Heaven, did the Boxer uprising take place. And even then there was almost no awareness of reality. The Boxer myths of invulnerability in the face of Western guns and of armies of countless "spirit soldiers" were a direct cause of their defeat. The self-image of the old China was only shattered on the rock of the Boxer Protocol.

The attitude of the United States toward the Chinese Empire was also one of moral superiority. The Americans had not waged war against China, but they had received the same privileges as the European powers. Nevertheless, they wished to draw a clear distinction between themselves and the "imperialists." This the American Government attempted to do through the Open Door notes. As we have seen, the circular memoranda of 1899 were little more than a free-trade "me too" claim, although those of 1900 made an unsuccessful effort to uphold the integrity of China. Yet the myth was established that, "in this episode of the Open Door notes, a tremendous blow had been struck for the triumph of American principles in international society—an American blow for an American idea."[29] Neither

[28] Griswold, *op. cit.*, p. 83.
[29] Kennan, *op. cit.*, p. 41.

their ineffectiveness nor American unwillingness to enforce them nor, moreover, Hay's departure from the goals set forth in them—"none of these things succeeded in shaking in any way the established opinion of the American public."[30] The Americans saw the Chinese as their wards and themselves as untainted by the nasty power politics of the Europeans. To America, the Open Door was a democratic policy guaranteeing equal opportunity to all and at the same time protecting the integrity of China. To China, the Americans had arrived late at the Western holdup, but just in time to share in the spoils. The door of China had never been opened voluntarily. Rather, it had been broken down.

The Boxer rising was never perceived in the United States as a legitimate nationalist movement. Rather, the Boxers were seen as criminals and fanatics. One contemporary American diplomat describes the edicts of the Empress Dowager as "the cruel decrees of a selfish ruler" and the uprising itself as "the barbarity of a frenzied mob."[31] Hence, when the Empire finally retaliated with force, the United States felt virtually betrayed by its protégé. So pervasive had the American self-image as the benevolent protector become that the Chinese attempt at self-assertion was met with fury. This explains why an American minister was able to order his troops to open fire on the Boxers "as an object lesson" and why another described the Boxer Protocol as "lenient." It also explains why the United States participated in the forceful suppression of the Boxer uprising.

Communist historians in China today explain the early relations between China and America in terms of a capitalist plot intended to victimize China. Communist China's image of those days is one of victimization at the hands of a great evil force invading China. In the words of a leading scholar, "this makes for self-pity, resentment, and the need for an explanation of history in terms of evil and injustice."[32] The foreign cannon of the Opium War and its aftermath boom more loudly in the ears of the present Communist leaders than they did in those of the apolitical peasants of the last century. The American response, on the other side of the gap, generally is a startled "Who, me?" when confronted with the historical data. The self-image of moral superiority coupled with one of benevolence toward China has persisted down to our own day.

Reflection shows that neither the American nor the Chinese images tally with the facts. No one-dimensional Communist devil theory showing

[30] *Ibid.*
[31] Williams, *op. cit.*, p. 423.
[32] John K. Fairbank, "Why Peking Casts Us as the Villain," *The New York Times Magazine*, May 22, 1966.

how American capitalism attacked, betrayed, and exploited the Chinese people, diverting their otherwise "normal development toward Communism," will do. Nor is the typical American textbook version of the period any more satisfactory. It is true that the Western impact was generally disastrous for China and that the United States was a part of that impact. However, this disaster was not the result of an imperialist plot, but rather of Western civilization expanding and coming into contact with the last remaining separate, distinct, and isolated empire in the world, an empire that conceived of itself as superior to all the others. Under this impact, the old China crumbled. As John K. Fairbank puts it succinctly and well: "Circumstances made China the worst accident case in history."[33] But the reciprocal images that accompanied these historical circumstances deepened the tragedy even further and made it echo down into the next century.

[33] Testimony of John K. Fairbank before the Committee on Foreign Relations, United States Senate, 89th Cong., 2nd Sess., *U. S. Policy With Respect to Mainland China* (Washington, D. C.: U. S. Government Printing Office, 1966), p. 102.

BENJAMIN I. SCHWARTZ

The Maoist Image of World Order

Are "The Chinese" prepared to accept the nation-state system that governs the international life of the West or are their images of the world and of China's place in it still governed by cultural habits derived from the remote past? It will be noted that this statement of alternatives leaves completely out of account a third category that dominates the discourse of the present Chinese Communist leadership itself—Marxism-Leninism and the "Thought of Mao Tse-tung." The latter is explicitly presented as marking a decisive break with both the culture of the past and the arrangements that govern the world of "capitalism and revisionism." Mao Tse-tung's present response to the above question no doubt would be a resounding rejection of both alternatives. We have, however, been educated by the profundities of the social sciences and depth psychology to discount conscious verbal behavior (at least on the part of others) in favor of larger "underlying" impersonal and unconscious forces. Nevertheless, in the following discussion the evolution of Communism in China will be treated as a third independent variable on the perhaps naïve assumption that what people say must be considered as at least one factor in explaining their behavior.

In dealing with non-Western societies we easily slip into the vulgar cultural anthropological mode. The notion that there is one easily defined and unchanging Chinese image of world order and that any given Chinese will embody this image is not likely to meet much resistance on the part of a

Benjamin I. Schwartz is professor of history and government at Harvard University, where he is associated with the East Asian Research Center. He is the author of *Chinese Communism and the Rise of Mao* and *In Search of Wealth and Power: Yen Fu and the West*.

Western audience. Just as any given Navaho chief is presumed to be a typical case of the unchanging patterns of Navaho culture, so Mao Tse-tung may be thought of as the incarnation of a uniform Chinese cultural response. In dealing with this question we have chosen to focus our attention on Mao Tse-tung not merely because he has obviously played a decisive role in recent Chinese history, but precisely in order to underline the fact that he is not the incarnation of a "Chinese image of world order" but one complex individual whose responses to many of the situations he has confronted have been signally different from those of other Chinese. As of this writing, we are indeed acutely aware that Mao's perceptions of many matters may differ most markedly even from those of some of his closest associates in the Chinese Communist leadership. Furthermore his life, like that of many of his contemporaries, illustrates not cultural stasis but the enormous cultural crisis that China has experienced in the twentieth century.

Traditional Chinese Image of World Order

Before dealing with Mao Tse-tung we must say something about the "traditional" Chinese image of world order. It must be stated candidly that those now making a serious effort to understand the history of Chinese culture tend to be profoundly uneasy about the simple and static generalizations which find such ready acceptance in these matters. In the West every generalization that we hazard about our international order must run the gauntlet of historians, specialists in international law, political theorists, and others, whereas generalizations about the millennial history of China still resound grandly in the vast cavern of our comparative ignorance. As our study of the Chinese past deepens, we will no doubt find that all of our present descriptions of the traditional order will undergo more and more qualification. Nevertheless, an attempt must be made.

In trying to discover the persistent features of the traditional image of world order, we find, first of all, the Chinese culture-area (*tien hsia*) conceived of as the center of a higher civilization that is ideally associated with a universal state governed by a universal king occupying a unique cosmic status. All surrounding states and principalities are ideally parts of this universal order and hierarchically subordinate to it in terms of tribute relationship. Of course such claims are not unique to China; they were made in ancient Mesopotamia, in Egypt, and in the Persian and Roman Empires. The uniqueness of the Chinese case lies in the persistence of such claims into the twentieth century. The Chinese universal kingship does not disappear from the scene until 1911.

The uniqueness of the Chinese experience does not necessarily spring from a particular cultural arrogance. It was in part due to certain contingent, external circumstances of Chinese history. In the ancient Middle East the absolute claims of Mesopotamian and Egyptian culture and universal kingship soon confronted each other. This fact may not have shaken Egyptian or Mesopotamian cultural confidence, but must certainly have done something to diminish the aura of these cultural and political claims among the various peoples who lived in surrounding and peripheral areas. China, on the other hand, remained unchallenged in its immediate vicinity by any polity whose cultural claims it felt obliged to consider. The only possible exception to this generalization is provided by Indian Buddhism. On the whole, however, Buddhism did not become the bearer of Indian political claims nor did it seriously challenge the basis of the Chinese universal kingship. The Chinese were not only unchallenged, they were also conscious of the influence of their own culture on surrounding peoples such as the Japanese, Vietnamese, and Koreans. And, as we know, "barbarian" rulers of China did tend in the long run to accept the absolute claims of the Chinese universal kingship. Thus experience tended to reinforce their claims.

One may, of course, raise questions about the degree to which the surrounding peoples accepted their assigned roles in the Chinese world order. The Japanese accepted cultural influence but managed to evade Chinese political claims. The Central Asian nomads and the peoples of Turkestan and Tibet probably never really accepted Chinese claims even where they were forced to assume the role of tribute bearers. Furthermore, there have been cases in the long history of China when emperors and officials have found it expedient to mute their own claims of political ascendancy. Still, if one considers the history of China in the last millennium in its broad sweep, it can be stated that the Chinese image of world order remained fundamentally intact.

It nevertheless may be asked how much this traditional Chinese image of the world order explains about the history of the foreign relations of the Chinese Empire. Does it, for instance, throw light on the question of Chinese aggressiveness? Actually, it was compatible with an extraordinarily wide range of attitudes and practices in the field of foreign policy. Surveying the long history of China one must arrive at the rather banal conclusion that it was compatible with both pacifistic isolationist policies and with aggressive expansionist policies. Even the attitude toward "barbarians" could run the gamut from the idealistic Mencian view that barbarians could be easily "civilized" by moral influence to the view that most of them were little better than beasts who could only be restrained by force. If Mao Tse-tung does indeed view the world through the eyes of his imperial predecessors, this throws little light on the future course of his policies. One would have to know which predecessors provide his model.

The traditional image probably had its most fateful effect on Chinese behavior during the nineteenth century, when it prevented an adjustment to the remorseless assault of the Western international system. The Chinese ruling class confronted a West as firmly committed to the universal validity of its conception of absolute nation-state sovereignty as the Chinese Empire was to its own view. Indeed, this conception had been given added weight by the rise of nineteenth-century nationalism. The history of China during the last half of the nineteenth century was marked by what Western observers regarded as an obscurantist, obdurate, and at times comical effort to resist the normal patterns of international relations. In retrospect it appears that the imperial court's resistance was probably based on an obscure yet sound instinct. The Chinese monarchy was, after all, inextricably tied to a cosmology of universal kingship. Whether it could have survived the crumbling of this cosmology and been converted into a Western-style "national" monarchy remains a moot point.

Chinese Nationalism and the Western Image

Despite this resistance, however, the striking fact remains that by the turn of the century many articulate Chinese had made the qualitative leap. They had come to accept the Western system with all its conventions and were prepared to think of China as one nation-state among others. Figures such as Yen Fu and Liang Chi-ch'ao, whose writings were to exercise an enormous influence on the generation of Chinese now in its seventies, were entirely prepared to jettison the traditional conception of China's place in the world as the price of China's survival as a political entity. They had not renounced China's greatness but were prepared to rethink it in terms of modern nationalism. This was true not only of nationalist revolutionaries such as Sun Yat-sen, but even of many of the intellectual leaders of the monarchist movement who had given up the commitment to universal kingship in favor of something like a national monarchy. For at least a small but decisive segment of China's population, the bases of the traditional conception of China's place in the world had decisively collapsed. Again, however, we must rid ourselves of the tyranny of cultural holism. This collapse did not necessarily involve a total break with the whole range of habits of thought and behavior inherited from the past. It was entirely possible for the same individual to accept the concept of China as a nation-state among others without abandoning other traditions. It was simply that this particular sector of the cultural heritage had proven itself peculiarly vulnerable to the assault of new experience. Traditionalists as well as Westernizers were committed to the survival of China as a political entity and were by now aware that its survival depended on the acceptance of the game as it was played in the West.

To be sure, even after the arrival of modern nationalism one can find a tendency among some Chinese intellectuals and politicians to speak of China's universal cultural contribution to mankind. Sun Yat-sen, a man without deep roots in the cultural heritage, became more and more insistent in his later years on China's universal mission and the contributions of Chinese civilization to mankind. Is such thinking to be regarded as a reversion to the Sinocentrism of the past or can it be explained as analogous to similar phenomena elsewhere? Nationalism everywhere displays a tendency to universalize the particular. The German will insist on the universal superiority of *Deutsche Kultur*, the French on their *"mission civilisatrice,"* and the Americans on the "American way of life." It used to be common to explain the transnational element in Soviet Communism in terms of Holy Russia's messianism and the doctrine of the third Rome. Admittedly, we are here in an area where the boundaries between all our well-defined categories become hazy. The only tangible method of dealing with this question, crude as it may be, is to ask whether the Chinese are prepared to play the game (loose and ambiguous as its rules are) in terms of the prevailing international system.

Chiang Kai-shek provides us with a good test case. Ever since the 1930's he has been much more insistent than Sun on the superiority of Chinese traditional values and their applicability to the problems of modern society. Whether this commitment is authentic or simply a manifestation of national pride—or both—I shall not presume to judge. Yet there is no evidence whatsoever that he has not accepted the nation-state system or not operated within its framework. His famous manifesto on "China's Destiny" (written under his imprimatur) is at once profoundly "traditionalistic" in tone and deep, even orthodox in its commitment to the principles of national sovereignty as defined in the West. In his conception of world order, he owes infinitely more to Bodin than to Confucius.

Turning to the biography of Mao Tse-tung, one can make a good case for the assertion that he has lived his life within a basically Chinese context, particularly if we hasten to add that the word "Chinese" refers not only to a changeless cultural heritage but to a twentieth-century China in crisis. The sensitive years of early childhood were spent in a rural society untouched by any direct Western influence, and his earliest view of the world was derived from Chinese sources. Again, it is important to note that these sources were by no means as homogeneous in their message as Westerners might think. The message he derived from his beloved Chinese epic novels was not precisely the same as that of the Four Books. One could even find in the heritage inspiration for rebelliousness. It will not do to speak of the traditional elements in Mao without attempting to define what these elements are. In spite of this "rootedness" in China, there is no reason to think that during his formative years of intellectual growth after 1910 Mao did not come to accept without reservation the Western image of world order. His knowledge of the world at large was wholly derived from the writings of Yen Fu, Liang Chi-ch'ao, and translations of Western writings, all of which simply assumed the premises of the nation-state system. The young pre-Communist Mao can be called a modern nationalist without the slightest reservation. Like many of his contemporaries he dreamt of China's resurgence, but of its resurgence as a great power in a world of great powers.

The Communist Dimension

Mao Tse-tung was to be converted to Marxism-Leninism, however, and with Marxism-Leninism we confront a new and complicating dimension. The October Revolution, as we know, was designed to shatter the whole "bourgeois" nation-state structure. Marx belonged to a whole group of nineteenth-century thinkers who regarded the international system of their time as anachronistic and moribund, and while we are all aware of the transformations that Marxism experienced at the hands of Lenin, there is every reason to believe that Lenin genuinely shared Marx's transnational outlook. In this he reflected the cosmopolitanism of a large sector of the Russian radical intelligentsia, which was quite unable to identify with the national glory of the Tsarist state. Lenin genuinely expected the October Revolution to serve as the spark for a world revolution that would dissolve the whole rotten international structure.

It is true that as a practical politician Lenin had devoted more attention to the "national question" than anyone else in the Marxist movement. He had created doctrinal rationalizations for harnessing resentful "bourgeois nationalism" to the wagon of revolution, and he had a genuine insight into the future role of such resentful nationalism in Asia. Lenin approached "bourgeois nationalism" from the outside as a cold manipulator, yet many of the formulae of Marxism-Leninism as they existed at the time of Lenin's death were already available for nationalist purposes. As a matter of fact, many of the young Chinese who were attracted to Marxism-Leninism in the early twenties (Mao among them) were already Chinese nationalists and as such were particularly attracted by those aspects of the Leninist theory of imperialism that seemed to explain China's national humiliation. This does not mean that they were completely insensitive to the apocalyptic cosmopolitan message of Communism. Indeed, some converts to Communism in China belonged to that small company of Chinese intellectuals who were ready to leap from the universalism of the older Chinese system to the transnational universalism of the new cosmopolitan philosophies from the West. The young Mao did not, on the whole, belong to their company. Surveying the evolution of his thought from 1921 to the present, one feels that Communism did not displace his nationalism but rather supplemented and complicated it.

In dealing with the relationship between "world Communism" and nationalism, we must first of all realize that we are not dealing with abstract essences but with a dynamic, evolving drama that has still not ended. It is a drama, moreover, in which the Chinese Communists themselves have played a large and ambiguous role.

In accepting Soviet Communism the Chinese Communists, including Mao, had of course accepted the notion of a supreme source of spiritual and political authority lying outside of China—this despite their nationalist passions. Furthermore, when this authority became completely tied to the interests of one territorial state—the Soviet Union—most of them continued to accept this authority. Only a handful of Chinese Trotskyists rejected the theory of "socialism in one country," and the supremacy of Moscow's authority in the Communist world continued to be accepted in Mao's China until the very end of the 1950's.

All of this has led some to suggest that the Chinese Communists, including Mao, in accepting the hierarchic superiority of the Soviet Union were in effect reverting to the hierarchic-vertical mode of thinking so characteristic of the traditional order and rejecting the unfamiliar Western notion of equally sovereign states. I find this notion difficult to accept. It is first of all quite clear, as we have noted, that the Western conception *had* been accepted without difficulty by many of the future members of the Communist Party. One of the main attractions of the Marxist-Leninist doctrine was that it provided a devastating critique of the arrogant imperialist West from a "modern" Western point of view. It provided an excellent way of dealing with the dilemma to which Mao referred retrospectively in his speech on "The People's Democratic Dictatorship" in 1949, namely, that "the teachers [the West] are constantly attacking their pupils." The young people who joined the party were probably much more conscious of the weapons it provided against Western *hybris* than of its implied subordination to Moscow.

There were, of course, other reasons why the formulae of Marxism-

Leninism proved attractive. Its assumption of knowledge regarding the direction of history, its promise of a total solution of China's immense problems of poverty, corruption, and disorganization must all be given great weight. I doubt very much that the attractions of the hierarchic concept of world order played a very significant role. It was, after all, a hierarchic order that placed the Chinese not at the summit but in an inferior position. The traditional order was based not on a mere abstract notion that there ought to be a hierarchic order in the relations of peoples, but on the rather specific complacent belief that China ought to be at the summit of this hierarchy. It would perhaps be more accurate to say that the Chinese Communists accepted Moscow's authority not because of the hierarchic implications of Soviet Communism but in spite of them. Their faith in certain basic assumptions of Marxism-Leninism was sufficiently strong to override their nationalist resistance.

This is particularly true, it seems to me, of Mao Tse-tung. He had accepted from Marxism-Leninism, as he understood it, many of the categories in terms of which the world is described; and many of these categories have continued to govern his image of the world to this very day. Until very recently this acceptance also involved a genuine acknowledgment of Moscow's ideological authority and of the Soviet Union as a model of socialism. It is precisely in this area, it seems to me, that a tension has existed from the very outset between the nationalist and transnationalist elements in his outlook.

We know of course that once he achieved ascendancy within the Chinese Communist movement during the Yenan period, he began to project his image of himself as the man who was applying the universal truths of Marxism-Leninism to the particularities of the Chinese situation. And he was doing this at a time when the doctrine was still dominant in Moscow that the authority to apply Marxist-Leninist doctrine to particular national situations was the exclusive prerogative of the Kremlin. We know that the nationalist coloration of Chinese Communism intensified during this period. In retrospect it does not seem at all plausible to assume that Mao Tse-tung was simply an "international Communist" manipulating Chinese nationalism from the outside. What is more probable is that he assumed that the aspirations of Chinese nationalism and of world Communism could be easily reconciled. He may have genuinely believed—even after 1949—that, whatever the difficulties, a Chinese Communist state would be able to maintain general harmony with the Soviet Union in terms of certain overriding shared beliefs, without renouncing any of its basic sovereign prerogatives as a nation-state. After Stalin's death, we know that the Chinese Communist

Government did everything possible to encourage those tendencies in Moscow that favored greater national autonomy within the world Communist movement; and since the outbreak of the Sino-Soviet conflict, the Chinese have, on one side of their polemic, made themselves the spokesmen of the most orthodox doctrine of national sovereignty within the Communist world. It is the Chinese who have promulgated one of the most striking doctrines in the whole church history of Communism, namely, that the decisions of any given national party (including the CPSU) are binding only within the area under the jurisdiction of that party.

All of this, of course, is highly "dialectic" in intention. One insists on the national sovereignty of states within the Soviet orbit in order to undermine the authority of the Soviet Union. Presumably, in a future international Communist order centered in Peking there will no longer be such insistence on national sovereignty. The fact remains that the Chinese Communist movement has itself played a crucial role in the unfolding relationship of Communism to nationalism. Whatever Mao's subjective intentions may be, Chinese Communism has helped to bring about what seems to be the triumph of the nation-state system over the transnational claims of Marxism-Leninism.

To be sure, in Peking the transnational aspirations now seem more alive than ever. The center of Communist authority, in Mao's view, has now definitely shifted from Moscow to Peking. True Marxism-Leninism is now dispensed only from Peking. It is thus precisely since the Moscow-Peking rift that those who emphasize the traditional cultural bases of Mao's image of the world have felt their case vindicated. Once again the Middle Kingdom has become the center of the "Way," and like the emperors of old, Mao Tse-tung is the highest source of both political authority and spiritual truth.

It is very difficult either to prove or to disprove a proposition of this nature. I have tried to demonstrate that both China and Mao Tse-tung have gone through a most tortuous course during the period between the collapse of the older world order and the present state of affairs, and that during that period many Chinese (including Mao at one stage in his life) had come to accept the nation-state framework without any difficulty, whatever their relationship may have been to other aspects of the traditional culture. The cosmology on the basis of which Mao asserts his authority is not the cosmology that underlay the traditional kingship. It is a cosmology that includes constant appeals to the authority of two "barbarians" named Marx and Lenin. It is of course true that the "Thought of Mao Tse-tung" is acquiring more and more weight within the ideological framework. Yet in appealing for support abroad the Chinese continue to emphasize the purity of their Marxism-Leninism. It may well be that this latest development in Chinese Communism resonates as it were with certain aspects of the traditional image of world order; however, the crucial question here is not whether it resonates with the traditional image but whether it is determined by it. If China's international behavior is determined by cultural images that have their roots in pre-history, we need not expect any speedy adjustments to a world that does not fit this image. If it is shaped by the more recent history of China and by a doctrine that is itself in a state of crisis and flux, if it is even shaped by the personal vision of Mao Tse-tung, who can in no way be equated with China, we must be alert to the possibility of sweeping shifts in the future.

Even as of this writing—in the very throes of the "cultural revolution"—China's relations with the world operate on two levels. On one level we find Mao's "higher" vision, in which China will be the center of a resurgent, purified Communist world. On another level we find the Chinese carrying on conventional diplomatic and commercial relations within the accepted nation-state framework, and even pressing the principle of national sovereignty within the Communist world. The aging Mao, to be sure, is deeply committed to his grand transnational vision and seems quite willing to sacrifice the possibility of more conventional diplomatic successes to the achievement of that vision.

These hopes for the realization of the vision, however, are not based on a programmatic blueprint but on certain expectations regarding the future course of world history. If these hopes are not realized in the foreseeable future, if the nation-state system proves as recalcitrant to the transnational hopes of Mao Tse-tung as it has to the hopes of others, will China be able to adjust to the world as it is? We have argued here that China has since the beginning of the twentieth century already demonstrated its ability to adjust to this system and that the process of adjustment has continued even under the Communists. Paradoxically, Mao Tse-tung has himself played a fateful role in weakening transnational authority within the Communist world. He has failed to consider the possibility that in undermining the supreme authority of Moscow in the Communist world he may have simply undermined the very notion of such authority in that world. Finally, there is now more room than ever for doubting whether all of Mao's colleagues within the Communist movement share the full ardor of his transnational vision.

I do not mean to suggest that the Western international system is more deeply rooted in some eternal, metahistorical order of things than the traditional Chinese conception of world order. In a world where China must continue to confront two other formidable world powers; in a world where there is an overriding passion for local and regional political independence; and in a world where none of the prevailing transnational ideologies, religions, or cultures have been able to establish their universal claims, the Western international system will continue to provide a more acceptable framework of world order than anything else available.

ROBERT C. NORTH

Perception and Action in the 1914 Crisis

The developing social-science approaches to history rest upon the fundamental assumption that there are patterns, repetitions, and close analogues throughout the record of human affairs. The circumstances and details will differ between the Peloponnesian War and World War I or World War II; but the sources, patterns, and generalized consequences of human anxieties, fears, and perceptions or expectations of threat, injury, or annihilation may not be dissimilar. A fundamental aspect of the problem lies in identifying the levels of abstraction where problems or events that are widely separated both in time and space may profitably be compared. We can identify almost endless differences between Carthage and Hiroshima, but both of these cities suffered wartime devastation. The weapons of annihilation were vastly different, but the dead of ancient Carthage were no less dead than the victims of atomic weaponry in Hiroshima. Nor do we have reason to believe that the basic human feelings, emotions, and decisions leading up to the two catastrophes—the fears, ambitions, greeds, anxieties, misperceptions, miscalculations, panics, and desperations—differ ignificantly.

There are outstanding advantages in using historical situations for this

Robert C. North is professor of political science and Director of the Studies in International Conflict and Integration at Stanford University. He is the author of *Moscow and Chinese Communists* and *Kuomintang and Chinese Communist Elites,* and a co-author of *Content Analysis: A Handbook with Applications for the Study of International Crisis.*

kind of research. With the whole sweep of recorded events to choose from, the scholar can select situations where the archives have been opened and where the documentation is relatively complete and illuminating. Obviously, it is impossible to acquire materials of this quality in more contemporary situations where security restrictions are enforced. The effort to develop a theory of international behavior will almost of necessity, then, rely heavily on the examination of evidence from the more distant past.

Historical situations offer the further advantage of an algebra book with answers in the back. Working with historical situations enables the social scientist to make "predictions" and to compare his "answers" with the way things actually turned out. He can compare in the minutest detail what statesmen have said with what they have done, and thus go a long way toward determining what perceptions have shaped their attitudes, intents, and decisions.

Indeed, for the study of international affairs we have no key to the future other than history that is available in one form or another. Human beings can scarcely judge what will happen in the future—or even assess the probable outcomes of their own choices and behaviors—except in terms of what has happened in the past. It is by comparing new problems and circumstances with old experience, identifying the similarities and differences, that we move toward the future. In general, we may assume that the more frequently and regularly things have happened in the past the greater the probability that they will happen in the future. Without occult prevision, human beings have no other way of assessing, judging, and deciding.

Foreign-policy decisions, like all other decisions, require not only abstraction from past experience, from history, but also the making of "predictions," that is, the assessment of probable outcomes. These two operations are often undertaken almost unconsciously, but they are nevertheless real and inescapable. With or without a crystal ball, we all make our decisions on the basis of prediction. The Marshall Plan was based on predictions, derived from some combination of past observation and experience, that systematic aid to the nations of Europe would bring about certain consequences. Viewed in retrospect, this prediction appears to have been sound. The basic prediction inherent in Khrushchev's decision to establish long-range missiles in Cuba, on the other hand, was much less accurate.

The six weeks immediately following the assassination of Austrian Archduke Francis Ferdinand offer an especially useful setting for examining the behavior of states in crisis, the processes of international conflict, and the spiraling of a limited war into a general war. Deeply embedded in the archival data lies something that approaches a prototype of international crisis, against which more contemporary crises can be measured with profit.

It is traditional and tempting to divide the "causes" of a great war into the fundamental and the immediate. The roots of any major conflict in modern times can always be traced far back into history. "Though it is now possible, in a single volume, to treat in detail and somewhat definitively the immediate cause of the War," Sidney B. Fay wrote in the introduction to his book, *The Origins of the World War*, "this is by no means true in the case of the underlying causes. These are so complex and reach so far back into the past that any attempt to describe them adequately would involve nothing less than the writing of the whole diplomatic history of Europe since 1870, or rather, 1789; since questions go back to the age of Louis XIV, and even to that of Charlemagne."[1] Indeed, almost everything that went before can be said to have a bearing, with the consequence that large arrays of diverse events are soon contending for recognition as major or minor causes. Moreover, to identify background trends or events as causal agents seems to impute an element of determinism that unfolding history may not warrant. It makes the outbreak of war, when it comes, appear inescapable, that is, beyond the capacity of any leadership to prevent.

Here our approach is somewhat different. In this paper we do not propose to discuss the underlying causes of war, although there is no question about their importance. We assume, however, that more or less serious conflicts are always present among nations and that it is possible for any one of a number of these to erupt into war. Indeed, between 1900 and 1914 there were several crises that seemed to carry European nations to the brink of large-scale violence, and yet in all cases but one the trend was at least momentarily reversed. What sets that one case apart? What distinguishes the 1914 crisis, which exploded into a major war, from the Bosnian Crisis of 1908 for example? Historical evidence suggests that although several of the European powers after the turn of the century thought that a major war was likely to occur sooner or later, and although some might have welcomed such a war in the longer run, none consciously planned or wanted the outbreak of hostilities in August 1914. Our focus, then, is upon the way a crisis is handled, upon how it is managed, rather than upon its origins—though we recognize the importance of historical perspective;

[1] Sidney Bradshaw Fay, *The Origins of the World War* (New York: The Macmillan Co., 1961).

the identification of persisting animosities, expectations, ambitions, and conflicts; and the context and circumstances from which the crisis emerged. More particularly, we want to find out how various leaders perceived these phenomena, which aspects they identified as threatening, what alternatives of action they saw confronting them—together with whatever available alternatives they may have failed to discriminate—and what the relationships were between perception and overt behavior.

The Outbreak of War in 1914

It is easy to forget that two wars broke out during the summer of 1914— one, which was intended to be localized, between Austria-Hungary and Serbia; and a second, which escalated from the first and became world-wide in its implications and involvements. In retrospect it appears that the world war was at least in part a consequence of miscalculations associated with the local conflict and of a kind of panic that seized certain leaders— especially the Kaiser—when, under extremely high tension, they felt themselves "surrounded" and hopelessly threatened.

In a six-week period of almost spiraling tension,[2] the interactions among the various states described a pattern that was somewhat more complex than a two-state model. Austria-Hungary's effort to relieve its sense of being threatened by punishing Serbia collided with Russia's determination to protect Serbia. When Russia mobilized to "deter" Austria-Hungary, Germany, under rising tension, perceived the troop movement as a threat to itself. In an effort to thwart the apparent threat ("self-protection" or "self-defense"), Germany invoked the Schlieffen Plan, which called for the invasion of Belgium. For England and France, in turn, the appearance of German troops in Belgium appeared threatening, and this apprehension incited them to take action to eliminate the perceived threat ("self-protection" or "self-defense").

The crisis began on June 28, 1914, when a young Serbian nationalist assassinated the Archduke Francis Ferdinand, heir apparent to the throne of Austria-Hungary, in the town of Sarajevo. Within a week Germany's Wilhelm II and his Imperial Chancellor, Bethmann-Hollweg, had promised virtual "blank check" support of Austria-Hungary in an action that was regarded as likely to eventuate in a "localized war" against Serbia.

[2] Tension is difficult to measure empirically and is therefore useful primarily in the development of theory. Techniques of measuring the various affects are described in Robert C. North, Ole R. Holsti, M. George Zaninovich, and Dina A. Zinnes, *Content Analysis: A Handbook with Applications for the Study of International Crisis* (Evanston, Ill.: Northwestern University Press, 1963). Research experience reveals that of all the affects hostility tends to be the most useful predictor of state behavior in crisis.

The concept of "localization" was central, since the German leaders were not consciously disposed to become involved in a major war at that time. It was recognized in Berlin that German military capabilities were inadequate, and the whole "blank check" policy rested on the assumption that the Russians, the French, and particularly the British would not intervene. In this respect the German leaders not only misperceived fundamental attitudes in St. Petersburg, Paris, and London, but persisted—almost to the eve of the major war—in the conviction that Russia would be constrained by the British and that the British, in turn, would maintain neutrality.

Later, when it became apparent in Berlin that these assessments were incorrect, both the Kaiser and the Chancellor felt suddenly "trapped" and were themselves incapable of foreseeing any alternative, any "way out," other than large-scale war. From this point the tension rose rapidly, with further distortions of perception at the time when crucial decisions were being made.

German Perceptions of Inadequate Strength

The historical record indicates that for at least two years prior to the outbreak of war German leaders had at their disposal persuasive evidence of the weakness of Germany and Austria-Hungary relative to the capabilities of Great Britain, France, and Russia.[3] According to the Chief of the General Staff, General von Moltke, writing in December 1912, a future war would threaten Germany's national survival.[4] Later—some three weeks after the Sarajevo assassination, but well before the Austro-Hungarian declaration of war on Serbia—Moltke dispatched to the German Chancellor a further warning, re-emphasizing German weaknesses and urging that universal military service be instituted immediately.

In disregarding these warnings, Austria and Germany did not overlook the possibly catastrophic outcome in the "unlikely" event that the local conflict should expand into a major war. Their leaders realized that in the existing circumstances a European war would be a "terrible calamity"[5]

---

[3] General Erich Ludendorff, *The General Staff and Its Problems: The History of the Relations between the High Command and the German Imperial Government as Revealed by Official Documents*, trans. by F. A. Holt (New York, n.d.), Vol. I, pp. 61, 64.

[4] Moltke to Bethmann-Hollweg. Germany, Reichsarchiv, *Der Weltkrieg 1914 bis 1918: Kriegsrusung and Kriegswirtschaft* (Berlin, 1930), supplement to Vol. I, No. 65, pp. 192-93.

[5] Protocol of the Council of Ministers for Common Concerns, July 7, 1914. Austro-Hungarian Monarchy, Ministerium des K. und K. Hauses und des Aeusseren, *Austrian Red Book: Official Files Pertaining to Pre-War History* (London, 1920), Vol. I, pp. 28-29. (Hereafter referred to as the *Austrian Red Book.*)

requiring "almost unbearable sacrifices and sufferings."[6] The outcome might well be "immeasurable."[7] Both Bethmann-Hollweg and Jagow, the German Secretary of State, referred more than once to the conflagration that might sweep the continent. The Kaiser, too, in a letter to the Czar, warned that an enlargement of the conflict might bring upon Europe "the most horrible war she ever witnessed."[8] And on July 29 the Grand General Staff submitted to the Chancellor a document that warned against "the mutual butchery of the civilized nations," a catastrophe that would "annihilate for decades the civilization of almost all Europe."[9]

German Perceptions of British, French, and Russian Intentions

It was essential to German policy, therefore, to keep the Austro-Serbian conflict strictly localized, which depended upon keeping the Russians, French, and British from intervening. This depended, in turn, upon the maintenance of close Anglo-German relations. With this in mind, it is perhaps strange that there was a strong predisposition in Berlin to take British neutrality and Anglo-German relations in general almost for granted.

On June 16, just prior to the assassination, Bethmann-Hollweg dispatched a confidential memorandum to the German Ambassador in London, Prince Lichnowsky. Keeping the peace in Europe depended almost exclusively upon the attitudes of Germany and England, the Chancellor asserted, and upon their cooperating in a common mission. " . . . I do not believe that Russia is plotting an early war against us. But she would doubtlessly like to do so. . . . " The essential thing was for England and Germany to "stand forth with determination" as the guarantors of European peace.[10]

At the July 5 meeting in which the German "blank check" was issued, Kaiser Wilhelm made his assumptions explicit. As reported by Admiral Tirpitz in his memoirs, the Kaiser believed that the Czar would not support "the assassins of royalty," and that Russia was militarily and financially unfit for war in any case. France, moreover, "would put the brake on

---

[6] The Hungarian Premier, Count Tisza, to the Emperor Franz Josef, July 8, 1914, *Austrian Red Book*, Vol. I, No. 12, p. 37.

[7] Count Berchtold to the Austro-Hungarian Ambassadors in St. Petersburg and Paris, July 29, 1914, *Austrian Red Book*, Vol. III, No. 15, p. 13.

[8] The Grand General Staff to Bethmann-Hollweg. *Outbreak of the World War: German Documents Collected by Karl Kautsky*, ed. by Max Montgelas and Walter Schücking (New York, 1924), p. 307. (Hereafter referred to as the *Kautsky Collection*.)

[9] *Ibid.*

[10] Bethmann-Hollweg to Lichnowsky, June 16, 1914, *Kautsky Collection*, pp. 55-56.

Russia, because of France's unfavorable financial position and her shortage of artillery. The Emperor did not mention England; there was no thought of complications with this State."[11]

From his post in London Ambassador Lichnowsky sent realistic dispatches to Berlin, and warned against counting too heavily on either British or Russian nonintervention. But Bethmann-Hollweg "had always considered that, if it came to war, England would certainly be neutral," and Jagow tried to reassure Lichnowsky in regard to St. Petersburg. "I readily believe your cousin Benckendorff when he says that Russia wants no war with us at present."[12] There was no doubt, according to the German Secretary of State, that Russia would be prepared to fight in a few years. "Then she will crush us . . . ." But for the time being St. Petersburg was "determined to have peace for a few years yet."[13]

For more than two weeks the conviction that there would be no intervention was repeated over and over again in Vienna and Berlin, and rationalized in the following fashion: There was no general disposition in Europe to sympathize with Serbia; Russia was beset with domestic difficulties and militarily unprepared; St. Petersburg was bluffing in its expressions of support for Serbia. As one German diplomat summed it up, "While the Russian likes to threaten with a sword, he still does not like so very much to draw it in behalf of others at the critical moment."[14] Jagow echoed that assessment in a dispatch to the London embassy on July 18: "The more determined Austria shows herself, the more energetically we support her, the more quiet will Russia remain. To be sure, there will be some agitation in Petersburg, but, on the whole, Russia is not ready to strike at present. Nor will France or England be anxious for war at the present time."[15]

The Russian Mobilization

It was against this background that Austria-Hungary, with German support and encouragement, on July 23 presented Serbia with a stern ultimatum calculated to provoke a rejection. Two days later, on July 25, Serbia

[11] Grand Admiral von Tirpitz, *My Memoirs* (London: Hurst and Blackett, Ltd., 1919), pp. 241-42.
[12] Jagow to Lichnowsky, July 18, 1914, *Kautsky Collection*, p. 132.
[13] *Ibid.*
[14] The Chargé d'Affairs [of Bavaria] in Berlin [Shoen] to the President of the [Bavarian] Ministerial Council, quoting Herr von Zimmerman, German Under-Secretary of State, July 18, 1914, *Kautsky Collection*, p. 618. See also Biedermann, the Saxon Chargé d'Affairs in Berlin, to the Minister of Foreign Affairs, Dresden, July 17, 1914, quoted in August Bach, *Deutsche Gesandtschaftsberichte zum Kriegsausbruch 1914* (Berlin: Quaderverlag g.m.b.h., 1937), pp. 64-66.
[15] Jagow to Lichnowsky, July 18, 1914, *Kautsky Collection*, p. 132.

responded with a note that, however conciliatory its intent, was viewed in Vienna as unsatisfactory. Both Serbia and Austria-Hungary began to mobilize, the Vienna government ordering into action eight (out of a total of sixteen) army corps. On July 28, the day of effective Austrian mobilization, the Vienna government declared war on Serbia.

Already there were rumors of rising Russian sympathies for the plight of Serbia, and German consular authorities in Warsaw, Riga, Kiev, and elsewhere reported local movements of Czarist troops. Yet German authorities continued to maintain their confidence in Russian—to say nothing of British—neutrality.

During the next two days, German leaders continued to underestimate Russian hostility toward Austria-Hungary for her action against Serbia —*up to a crucial threshold point*. Thereupon, Berlin misperceived Russian moves undertaken in order to deter Austria as moves specifically threatening to Germany. This perception of a Russian threat, moreover, seemed to tap reservoirs of deep, at least partially subconscious, German resentment against and fear of England—to the extent that Berlin overreacted spectacularly to what appear in retrospect as relatively mild and restrained expressions of disapproval and hostility from London.

The German Ambassador in St. Petersburg, Count de Pourtalès, had reported on July 27 that Russian officials were "breathing easier" and "striving to find a way out" of supporting Serbia by overt action.[16] This reassurance reached the German Foreign Office on July 29, and was forwarded to the Kaiser on July 30.

On returning to Berlin on July 27, the British Ambassador, Sir Edward Goschen, had reported back to London: "I found Jagow ill and tired but nevertheless optimistic—his optimism being based, as he told me, on the idea that Russia was not in a position to make war."[17]

The Kaiser also was still optimistic. At the time of the July 25 Serbian reply to the Austrian ultimatum, Wilhelm had been aboard his yacht cruising in the North Sea, and he did not see the actual text until the morning of July 28.[18] After reading the Serbian reply, he dispatched a memorandum to his Secretary of State: " . . . I am convinced that on the whole the wishes of the Danube Monarchy have been acceded to . . .

[16] Pourtalès to Bethmann-Hollweg, July 27, 1914, *Kautsky Collection*, p. 300.

[17] *British Documents on the Origins of the War, 1898-1914*, ed. by G. P. Gooch and Harold Temperley (London: His Majesty's Stationery Office, 1926), Vol. XI, p. 677.

[18] Tirpitz, *Memoirs*, p. 259. According to Admiral Tirpitz, the Kaiser was not alone in his lack of information at this time. "Jagow was so little interested in the Austro-Serbian conflict that he confessed to the German Ambassador on July 27th that he had not yet found time to read the Serbian reply to Austria."

Serbia has been forced to retreat in a very humiliating manner, and we offer our congratulations. Naturally, as a result, EVERY CAUSE FOR WAR HAS VANISHED. But a GUARANTY that the promises WILL BE CARRIED OUT is unquestionably necessary . . . ."[19] Yet disturbing reports from Russia continued to come in: Shortly after noon that same day a wire from the German General Consulate in Moscow reported that mobilization was "alleged to be in process."[20]

On the evening of July 29 the Kaiser telegraphed the Czar his "gravest concern" over the impression that "the action of Austria against Serbia" was creating in Russia. The "outrageous crime" at Sarajevo was an outcome of the "unscrupulous agitation" that had been taking place in Serbia for years.

> . . . on the other hand I fully understand how difficult it is for you and your Government to face the drift of your public opinion. Therefore, with regard to the hearty and tender friendship which binds us both from long ago with firm ties, I am exerting my utmost influence to induce the Austrians to deal straightly to arrive at a satisfactory understanding with you. I confidently hope you will help me in my efforts to smooth over difficulties that may still arise.
>
> Your very sincere and devoted friend and cousin,
> Willy[21]

Approaching the "Upper Limits"

On July 29, the day following the Austro-Hungarian declaration of war, Imperial Russia, acting in support of a small, fellow-Slav nation, ordered —and then cancelled—a general mobilization; it was later decided that mobilization would be directed only against Austria-Hungary.

The German Ambassador at St. Petersburg, Pourtalès, reported the Russian view to the Berlin Foreign Office during the afternoon of July 29: Austria had "mobilized eight corps, and this measure must be regarded as in part directed against Russia. As a result Russia found herself compelled to mobilize the military districts on the Austrian frontier." Pourtalès, according to his report, took issue with the Russian view, pointing out that "the danger of every preparatory military measure lay in the countermeasures of the other side."[22]

[19] The Emperor to Jagow, July 28, 1914, *Kautsky Collection*, p. 273. Capitalization in the source.

[20] The Administrator of the General Consulate in Moscow to the Foreign Office, July 27, 1914, *Kautsky Collection*, p. 274.

[21] The Emperor to the Czar, July 28, 1914, *Kautsky Collection*, pp. 296-97.

[22] Pourtalès to the Foreign Office, July 29, 1914, *Kautsky Collection*, p. 303.

At 3:15 p.m. on the same day the Berlin Foreign Office received a telegram from the German Military Plenipotentiary in St. Petersburg:

> Up to yesterday all the *entourage* of the Emperor [Czar] were filled with the hope of a peaceful outcome; today, since the declaration of war [against Serbia], they consider a *general* war almost *inevitable* . . . .

The Plenipotentiary proceeded to assert, however, that "*They do not want war . . .* ," and upon reading the telegram Wilhelm underscored these words twice.[23]

In the meantime, British policy—even for two days after the Austrian ultimatum and up to the evening of July 29—had been characterized largely by inaction.[24] If Germany and Austria persisted in the assumption that Britain, France, and Russia would not intervene, it was equally true that none of these countries had made its interests, predispositions, and limits clear, though Prince Lichnowsky had rather consistently reported his personal conviction that English neutrality could not by any means be taken for granted.

On learning that the Serbian reply to the Austrian ultimatum was being drawn up "in the most conciliatory terms," the British Foreign Secretary, Sir Edward Grey, communicated to Prince Lichnowsky on July 25 the "hope that if the Serbian reply when received in Vienna corresponds to this forecast [of conciliation], the German Government may feel able to influence the Austrian Government to take a favorable view of it."[25]

The Kaiser's reaction to British suggestions for an extension of the time limit imposed on Serbia by Austria and for mediation by the major powers was contained in a marginal note in Wilhelm's handwriting:

> Useless. This is superfluous, as Austria has already made matters plain to Russia and Grey has nothing else to propose. I will not join it unless Austria expressly asks me to, which is not likely. In vital questions and those of honor, one does not consult with others.[26]

It was not until 6:39 p.m. of July 29 that Prince Lichnowsky telegraphed Berlin a warning from Sir Edward Grey. The British Foreign Minister, "calm but very grave," had noted that the situation was growing more acute. He repeated his earlier suggestion for mediation: it was "urgently

---

[23] The Military Plenipotentiary at the Russian Court to the Foreign Office, July 29, 1914, *Kautsky Collection*, p. 304. Emphasis in the source.

[24] See Luigi Albertini, *The Origins of the War of 1914* (London: Oxford University Press, 1953), Vol. II, pp. 329-45 and 508-22.

[25] *British Documents*, p. 115.

[26] *Kautsky Collection*, pp. 184-85.

necessary if *a European* catastrophe were not to result." Grey then urged upon Lichnowsky "a friendly and private communication":

> The British Government desires now as before to cultivate our previous friendship, and it could *stand aside as long as the conflict remained confined to Austria and Russia*. But if we and France should become involved, then the situation would immediately be altered, and the British Government would, *under the circumstances find itself forced to make up its mind quickly*. In that event *it would not be practicable to stand aside and wait for any length of time*.

It was far from his desire to express any kind of threat, the Foreign Minister asserted. He wanted only to protect Prince Lichnowsky from disappointments and himself from the reproach of bad faith. "If war breaks out," Lord Grey declared, "it will be *the greatest catastrophe* that the world has ever seen."[27] Lichnowsky's warning reached the German Foreign Office at 9:12 p.m. July 29, but the decoded text was not submitted to Kaiser Wilhelm until 1 p.m. the following day.

By 6 a.m. of July 30 Bethmann-Hollweg was submitting a report of the Russian mobilization against Austria to Kaiser Wilhelm. He stressed Russian assurances that this decision did not mean war at all and that, in any case, "no mobilization had in any way taken place against Germany."

But tensions in Berlin were now rising rapidly, and these hours marked the beginning of Wilhelm's growing panic. "According to this the Czar has simply been tricking us with his appeal for assistance and has deceived us," the Kaiser noted in the margins of the document at 7 a.m. ". . . Then I must mobilize, too." The Czar had "simply lied," mobilizing behind the Kaiser's back. " . . . the hope that I would not let his mobilization measures disturb me in my role of mediator is childish, and solely intended to lure us into the mire. I regard my mediation action as brought to an end . . . ."[28]

Up to this point the tensions in Berlin had been relatively vague, diffuse, and unfocused. The Kaiser and his colleagues had felt themselves, and more particularly Austria, to be the target of hostility and threats, but the source had never been clearly identified in their thoughts other than in terms of Serbian lawlessness and an ill-defined Pan-Slavism. But from now on the Kaiser seemed to lunge out—almost desperately and blindly—in efforts to identify enemies.[29]

---

[27] Lichnowsky to the Foreign Office, July 29, 1914, *Kautsky Collection*, pp. 321-22. Italics in the source.
[28] Bethmann-Hollweg to the Emperor, July 30, 1914, *Kautsky Collection*, p. 347.
[29] German perceptions of hostility reached a peak between July 30 and August 1.

Meanwhile, technical difficulties were causing the Russian Government to reverse its decision in favor of general mobilization once again, German warnings notwithstanding. The Czar explained the new Russian activities in a telegram to the Kaiser:

> . . . The *military measures which have now come into force were decided five days ago for reasons of defense on account of Austria's preparations.* I hope from all my heart that these measures *won't in any way interfere* with your part as mediator which I greatly value. *We need your strong pressure on Austria* to come to an *understanding with us.*
>
> Nicky

Again Wilhelm added his own comments.

> . . . these measures are for DEFENSE against AUSTRIA, which is *in no way* attacking him ! ! ! I cannot agree to any more mediation, since the Czar who requested it has at the same time mobilized behind my back. It is only a maneuver, in order to hold us back and to increase the start they have already got. My work is at an end.[30]

It was now 1:20 p.m. in Berlin. Only twenty minutes earlier Lord Grey's warning had reached the Kaiser's desk: "If war breaks out, it will be the *greatest catastrophe* that *the world has ever seen.*" In the margin opposite this sentence Wilhelm wrote, "This means they will attack us." Lord Grey, he added, had "shown bad faith all these years . . . . " And opposite Prince Lichnowsky's report of the British Foreign Secretary's concern to "spare himself later the reproach [of] bad faith" the Kaiser scribbled, "Aha! The common cheat."[31]

In a note at the end of the telegram Wilhelm added, in part: "England reveals herself in her true colors at a moment when she thinks that we are caught in the toils and, so to speak, disposed of. That common crew of shopkeepers has tried to trick us . . . Grey proves the King a liar, and his words to Lichnowsky are the outcome of an evil conscience, because he feels that he has deceived us." England was combining threat with bluff "to separate us from Austria and to prevent us from mobilizing, and to shift the responsibility of the war." Grey knew perfectly well that one sharp word in Paris and St. Petersburg would keep them quiet and neutral, but he was threatening Germany instead. "Common cur! England alone bears the responsibility for peace and war, not we any longer . . . . "[32]

---

[30] The Czar to the Emperor, July 30, 1914, *Kautsky Collection*, p. 342. Emphasis in the source.

[31] *Kautsky Collection*, p. 321. Emphasis in the source.

[32] *Ibid.*, p. 322.

On a memorandum from Bethmann-Hollweg the Kaiser noted at 1:30 p.m. his receipt of a telegram that morning from the German naval attaché in London to the effect that, " . . . in case we went to war against France England would *immediately proceed* to attack us at sea with her fleet."[33]

Meanwhile, during the early morning hours the Russian Minister of Foreign Affairs, Sazonov, had told Count Pourtalès why the order for full mobilization, which he said was necessitated by the Austrian mobilization, could "no longer possibly be retracted."[34] Pourtalès filed a report of this conversation at 4:30 a.m., and in due course it was forwarded to the Kaiser, who noted the hour—"7 o'clock in the evening"—and added extensive marginal comments.

There was no doubt left about it: England, Russia, and France had agreed among themselves—after laying the foundation of *casus foederis* through Austria—to wage a war of extermination against Germany. The circumscription of Germany had finally become a fact, and frivolity and weakness were to plunge the world into a most frightful war aimed at German destruction. "The net has been suddenly thrown over our head, and England sneeringly reaps the most brilliant success of her persistently prosecuted purely *anti-German world policy*, against which we have proved ourselves helpless, while she twists the noose of our political and economic destruction out of our fidelity to Austria, as we squirm *isolated* in the net." From the dilemma raised by "our fidelity to the venerable old Emperor of Austria" Germany had been brought into a situation that offered England "the desirable pretext of annihilating us under the hypocritical cloak of justice . . . ," stirring "all the European nations in England's favor against us!"

Previously the Kaiser and his colleagues had persistently misperceived British, French, and Russian attitudes and intentions. Now, in the course of a few hours, they swung to the other extreme: exaggerating British, French, and Russian hostilities and grossly overreacting. In the consequent high tension, moreover, they were unable to see any alternatives to large-scale war. "This whole business must now be ruthlessly uncovered," the Kaiser asserted, "and the mask of Christian peaceableness publicly and brusquely torn from its face in public, and the pharisaical hypocrisy exposed on the pillary!!" The time had come to strike back, not only in Europe but throughout the world. German consuls and other agents in Turkey, India, and elsewhere "must fire the whole Mohammedan world to

[33] *Ibid.*, p. 354. Emphasis in the source.
[34] Pourtalès to the Foreign Office, July 30, 1914, *Kautsky Collection*, p. 349.

fierce rebellion against this hated, lying, conscienceless nation of shop-keepers; for if we are to be bled to death, England shall at least lose India."[35]

On July 31 Germany proclaimed a "state of threatening danger of war" and dispatched a twelve-hour ultimatum to Russia, demanding a cessation of preparations on the German frontier. At this peak of tension neither the Kaiser nor his opponents could perceive feasible alternatives, despite British proposals for negotiation. The German leaders were incapable of seeing any other "way out." On the next day Berlin ordered mobilization and, at 7 p.m., declared war on Russia, which had not replied to the ultimatum.

Foreseeing a two-front war—against Russia to the East and France to the West—Germany sought to gain an initial advantage by invading Luxembourg and submitting to Belgium a demand that she be permitted to cross Belgian territory. On August 3 Berlin declared war against France, and on August 4 Great Britain declared war against Germany.

In the space of six weeks a seemingly localized dispute in the Balkans had grown into a European conflict, and over the succeeding years the greater part of the world became involved. At almost every major turning point the men who made the crucial decisions were strongly affected by essentially emotional, non-rational phenomena.[36] When the fighting finally came to an end in 1918, the Austro-Hungarian Monarchy was in a state of dissolution, and the Kaiser's Germany on the point of collapse.

Such, in sketchy outline, was the sequence of events that we shall now consider in terms of the content analysis performed on the basic decision-making documents.

Content Analysis of Perceptions and Actions

The perceptual data were derived from documents written between June 27 and August 4 by key British, German, French, Russian, and Austro-Hungarian leaders able to commit the resources of their respective states to the pursuit of foreign-policy goals. All the available documents in this category were coded.

The first problem in using these documents was to decide upon perceptual units that could be defined, recognized by separate investigators, counted, and ranked according to their degree of intensity. The units decided upon—the *perceptions*—have been abstracted from the documents in terms of the following elements: *the perceiving party or actor; the per-*

---

[35] *Kautsky Collection*, p. 350.
[36] Cf. Thomas W. Milburn, "The Concept of Deterrence: Some Logical and Psychological Considerations," *The Journal of Social Issues*, Vol. XVII, No. 3, pp. 3-11.

ceived party or actor; the action or attitude; and the target party or actor. The 1914 documents yielded over five thousand cognitive and affective perceptions. [37]

There were three stages of analysis: (1) using *frequency* of perception only; (2) recoding the documents and scaling the perceptions according to the *intensity* of various attributes; and (3) correlational analyses between perceptions and various types of *"hard"* and *action* data. An initial paper, using frequency of themes as a technique of analysis, tested two basic hypotheses about the relationships between perceptions of threat and perceptions of capability in an international crisis.[38] In his analysis of the decision to go to war, including the case of 1914, Theodore Abel concluded that "in no case is the decision precipitated by emotional tensions, sentimentality, crowd behavior, or other irrational motivations."[39] The evidence presented in that initial study strongly suggested a contrary hypothesis: *Perceptions of one's own inferior capability, if anxiety, fear, or perceptions of threat or injury are intense enough, will fail to deter a nation from going to war.*

Using perceptual data—but no action data—from the 1914 crisis, Dina A. Zinnes tested four hypotheses about the relationships between perceptions of hostility and expressions of hostility by key decision-makers.[40] In the 1914 case it was found that a nation-state tends to reciprocate hostility to the degree that it sees itself to be the target of another state's hostility.

[37] For a full description of this technique of handling data see Robert C. North *et al.*, *op. cit.* The reliability coefficient $R = \dfrac{2\;(C_{1,\;2})}{C_1 \;+\; C_2}$ used in this coding of perceptions required not only that all coders pick up the same number of statements, but also that they agree on the identity of each statement. The composite reliability for the various categories of perceptions gathered—hostility, friendship, frustration, satisfaction, etc.—was .67. The reliability for coding hostility was considerably higher, reaching .80 and better, according to the training of the coders. But the composite .67 level is a more accurate indication of the limitations of the coding technique.

[38] Dina A. Zinnes, Robert C. North, and Howard E. Koch, Jr., "Capability, Threat, and the Outbreak of War," *International Politics and Foreign Policy*, ed. by James N. Rosenau (New York: The Free Press of Glencoe, 1961).

[39] Theodore Abel, "The Element of Decision in the Pattern of War," *American Sociological Review*, Vol. VI (1941), pp. 853-59.

[40] Dina A. Zinnes, "Expression and Perception of Hostility in Inter-State Relations," Ph.D. dissertation, Stanford University, 1963. The following four hypotheses were tested: (1) *if x perceives itself the object of hostility, then x will express hostility;* (2) *if x perceives itself the object of y's hostility, then x will express hostility toward y;* (3) *if x expresses hostility toward y, then y will express hostility toward x;* (4) *if y expresses hostility toward x, then x will express hostility toward y.* The correlations for the third and fourth hypotheses were negative, perhaps as a function of the research model.

These studies reinforced the belief that content analysis of documentary material provides a rich source of data. They also demonstrated the importance of measuring the intensity as well as the frequency of perceptions. The entire set of documents was therefore recoded and all perceptions, after masking, were rated according to the intensity of hostility, friendship, frustration, satisfaction, and desire to change the status quo on a scale of 1 to 9 by the Q-Sort technique.[41] The quantitative results were then aggregated into twelve time periods, each containing approximately one-twelfth of the documentation.

When the hypotheses relating perceptions of capability and threat were re-examined, it was found that the decision-makers of each nation felt themselves to be threatened at the time when they were making policy decisions of the most crucial nature.[42] Perceptions of its inferior capability did not deter a nation like Germany from going to war. The Kaiser's desperate response to the events that were engulfing him suggests the behavior of a decision-maker under stress so severe that any action is preferable to the burden of the sustained tension.[43]

Such behavior in the face of an adversary's greater capability—strikingly similar to instances in the Peloponnesian War, the wars between Spain and England during the sixteenth century, and the Japanese decision to strike at Pearl Harbor[44]—is by no means unrelated to our age of nuclear warheads and missiles. These findings underscore the need for re-examining that "common sense" and almost irresistible "conventional wisdom" that argues that deterrence is merely a matter of piling up more and better weapons than one's opponent.

Scholars in the field of international relations have frequently asserted that nations acting in crisis situations reveal more or less consistent patterns of rising tensions and escalating conflict leading to war.[45] The basic proposition can be stated as follows: If state A—correctly or incorrectly—per-

---

[41] Jack Block, *The Q-Sort Method in Personality Assessment and Psychiatric Research* (Springfield, Ill.: Charles C. Thomas, 1961).

[42] Ole R. Holsti and Robert C. North, "The History of Human Conflict," *The Nature of Human Conflict*, ed. by Elton B. McNeil (Englewood Cliffs, N. J.: Prentice-Hall, Inc., 1965).

[43] These findings appear to support Russett's assumption that "the outbreak of war, at least on a scale involving several major powers, was an accident rather than the result of a deliberate aggressor's plot." See Bruce M. Russett, "Cause, Surprise and No Escape," *The Journal of Politics,* Vol. XXIV (1962), p. 4. This does not preclude the possibility of "accident proneness."

[44] Ole R. Holsti, "The Value of International Tension Measurement," *The Journal of Conflict Resolution,* Vol. VII (1963), pp. 608-17.

[45] See Kenneth E. Boulding, *Conflict and Defense* (New York: Harper & Bros., 1962); and Lewis F. Richardson, *Arms and Insecurity* (Chicago: Quadrangle Books, 1960).

ceives itself threatened by state B, there is a high probability that A will respond with threats of hostile action. As state B begins to perceive this hostility, it is probable that B, too, will behave in a hostile (and defensive) fashion. This threatening behavior by B will convince A that its initial perceptions were correct, and A will be inclined to increase its hostile (and defensive) activity. Thereafter, the exchanges between the two parties will become increasingly negative, threatening, and injurious.[46]

An initial and partial test of this proposition was carried out by correlating perceptual or affective data from 1914 with the spiral of military mobilizations just prior to the outbreak of World War I.[47] The findings suggest that mobilizations were accounting for a considerable part, though by no means all, of the variance of the hostility. There was a steady rise in hostility prior to any acts of mobilization, and thus the decision-makers were to some degree responding to verbal threats and diplomatic moves, rather than to troop movements, in the earlier phases of the crisis. This study thus revealed the necessity of correlating perceptual data with other types of action data. (It also underscored the importance of testing hypotheses in other crisis situations, since there was little in the 1914 data to suggest under what conditions the exchange of threats leads to "de-escalation," rather than to a conflict spiral, as appears to have happened in the October 1962 Cuban crisis.)

The action data were expanded to include all events of a military character involving nations in the 1914 crisis either as agents or targets of actions. These were gathered from standard military histories of the period[48] and such usually reliable newspapers as *The New York Times*, *The Times* (London) and *Le Temps*. Wherever possible the reports were verified in an authoritative history of the crisis.[49] These sources yielded 354 military events. The action data were also scaled by Q-Sorting according to the degree of violence.[50] A summary of the action data, both

[46] Robert C. North, "International Conflict and Integration: Problems of Research," *Intergroup Relations and Leadership*, ed. by Muzafer Sherif (New York: John Wiley and Sons, Inc., 1962).

[47] Robert C. North, Richard A. Brody, and Ole R. Holsti, "Some Empirical Data on the Conflict Spiral," *Peace Research Society (International) Papers*, Vol. I, 1964.

[48] Sir James E. Edmunds, *Official History of the War, Military Operations: France and Belgium 1914*, 3rd ed. (London: Macmillan and Co., 1937); Girard L. McEntee, *Military History of the World War* (New York: Scribner's, 1937); and Thomas C. Frothingham, *The Naval History of the World War: Offensive Operations, 1914-1915* (Cambridge: Harvard University Press, 1924).

[49] Albertini, *op. cit.*

[50] For a technique of scaling action data that bypasses some of the difficulties inherent in the Q-Sort (e.g., the non-comparability of two independent samples) see Lincoln E. Moses, Richard A. Brody, Ole R. Holsti, Joseph B. Kadane, and Jeffrey S. Milstein, "Scaling Inter-Nation Action Data" (Stanford University, 1966).

in terms of frequency and intensity, for the entire crisis is found in Table 1. Unless the target of an action was explicit (e.g., "Austrian artillery units bombarded Belgrade"), the target was designated as "general."

For purposes of combining action and perceptual data, the perceptual materials were operationalized solely in terms of the hostility variable. Previous studies involving multivariant analysis, which have revealed hostility to be the best predictor of action, were supported in the present

TABLE 1.

Summary Table of Action Data

TARGET

AGENT	Austria-Hungary	Germany	England	France	Russia	Serbia	All Others	General	Total
Austria-Hungary	0.00 (0)	0.00 (0)	0.00 (0)	0.00 (0)	4.50 (1)	6.33 (29)	6.00 (1)	5.43 (23)	5.01 (54)
Germany	0.00 (0)	0.00 (0)	5.50 (4)	6.81 (16)	6.00 (11)	4.75 (2)	6.00 (4)	4.62 (57)	5.26 (94)
England	0.00 (0)	6.25 (4)	0.00 (0)	0.00 (0)	0.00 (0)	0.00 (0)	7.00 (1)	4.38 (36)	4.62 (41)
France	0.00 (0)	5.00 (13)	0.00 (0)	0.00 (0)	0.00 (0)	0.00 (0)	0.00 (0)	3.84 (51)	4.08 (64)
Russia	6.43 (7)	6.29 (7)	0.00 (0)	1.00 (1)	0.00 (0)	0.00 (0)	0.00 (0)	5.31 (35)	5.52 (50)
Serbia	4.64 (7)	0.00 (0)	0.00 (0)	0.00 (0)	4.00 (1)	0.00 (0)	2.50 (1)	5.94 (8)	5.09 (17)
All Others	0.00 (0)	0.00 (0)	0.00 (0)	0.00 (0)	0.00 (0)	7.00 (1)	0.00 (0)	4.30 (33)	4.38 (34)
Total	5.54 (14)	5.58 (24)	5.50 (4)	6.47 (17)	5.73 (13)	6.25 (32)	5.64 (7)	4.60 (243)	5.01 (354)

Top number is average intensity
Number in parentheses is frequency

TABLE 2.

Intensity Level of Perceptual and Action Variables—Dual Alliance and Triple Entente

	6/27-7/2	7/3-7/16	7/17-7/20	7/21-7/25	7/26	7/27	7/28	7/29	7/30	7/31	8/1-8/2	8/3-8/4
Hostility:												
Dual Alliance	3.46	3.63	3.79	4.13	4.84	4.09	4.83	4.99	5.50	5.80	6.89	6.42
Triple Entente	3.67	4.22	4.00	4.25	5.07	4.93	5.61	5.42	5.44	5.58	5.70	6.10
Friendship:												
Dual Alliance	4.79	5.22	4.19	4.61	5.27	5.17	5.60	4.85	5.25	5.95	5.53	4.95
Triple Entente	0.00	6.10	6.00	5.00	4.50	4.10	4.64	4.40	4.77	5.23	4.24	5.46
Frustration:												
Dual Alliance	4.93	4.45	3.90	5.33	5.97	4.62	4.49	4.65	5.84	6.22	4.39	6.00
Triple Entente	3.33	4.60	4.33	5.50	4.83	5.46	4.78	5.19	4.78	4.61	4.78	4.42
Satisfaction:												
Dual Alliance	2.91	5.83	4.05	2.58	5.33	4.83	3.33	0.00	4.67	5.90	6.00	5.83
Triple Entente	0.00	5.25	5.67	4.22	4.83	4.55	6.17	4.95	5.00	6.00	5.47	6.21
Change Status Quo:												
Dual Alliance	6.45	5.27	4.92	4.89	4.42	4.49	4.79	4.85	5.46	5.55	5.51	5.71
Triple Entente	5.25	3.75	4.72	4.80	4.74	4.51	4.75	4.88	4.58	4.77	4.81	5.17
Violent Behavior:												
Dual Alliance	4.25	3.00	2.83	5.38	5.37	5.87	6.06	4.64	5.10	6.30	5.58	6.08
Triple Entente	4.38	2.58	2.62	4.28	3.68	4.95	4.68	5.07	4.60	5.50	5.90	6.03

Correlations (N = 24)

	Viol.	C.S.Q.	Sat.	Frust.	Frsp.
Hostility	.643*	.045	.482#	.353	.272
Friendship	.060	-.199	.605+	.424#	
Frustration	-.415#	-.029	.315		
Satisfaction	.117	-.169			
Change Status Quo	.146				

Significance Level: * = .001 + = .01 # = .05

Partial Correlation Coefficients
of Independent Variables with
Violence as Dependent Variable:

Hostility	.636+
Friendship	-.103
Frustration	-.236
Satisfaction	.348
Change Status Quo	.093

study. With violence of action as the dependent variable, only the partial correlation coefficient for hostility ($r = .636$) is statistically significant (Table 2).[51]

For the Triple Entente, which became involved relatively late in the crisis, the level of overt response was generally congruent with, or more or less appropriate to, the level of environmental stimulus. The Dual Alliance, on the other hand, tended to respond on a level of violence somewhat higher than might be considered appropriate for the environmental stimulus. A relatively high level of negative emotion or affect seemed to account for this discrepancy, the leaders of the Dual Alliance tending to exaggerate the threats and overreact to them.

[51] Extensive correlational and multiple regression analyses of all perceptual variables have been made against various types of independent behavioral data. The latter include a pre-scaled chronology of the 1914 crisis, a series of key economic indicators, and mobilization data. Each analysis revealed that hostility is clearly the variable most sensitive to behavioral change.

RALPH K. WHITE

Misperception of Aggression in Vietnam

In the Vietnam war each side declares that it has to fight because of obvious, self-evident "aggression" by the other side. On each side there are images of a Hitler-like enemy, brutally, calculatingly bent on conquest. On each side there is a feeling that it would be weak and cowardly to let the enemy's aggression be rewarded by success; each side feels: "If we are men we cannot let this aggression go unpunished."

The thesis of this article is that both are wrong. There has been no aggression on either side—at least not in the sense of a cold-blooded, Hitler-like act of conquest. The analogies of Hitler's march into Prague, Stalin's takeover of Eastern Europe, and the North Korean attack on South Korea are false analogies. There is a better analogy in the outbreak of World War I, when, as historical scholarship has shown, both sides stumbled and staggered into the war in a spirit of self-defense (or defense of national pride against "intolerable humiliation") rather than in a spirit of deliberate conquest. (See Robert North's article in this issue.) In Vietnam each side, though by no means free from moral guilt, is far from being as diabolical as its enemies picture it, since both believe that whatever crimes they may commit are justified by the magnitude of the emergency. Each knows that

Ralph K. White is professor of psychology and a member of the Institute for Sino-Soviet Studies at George Washington University. He is the co-author of *Autocracy and Democracy: An Experimental Inquiry*. His study of "Images in the Context of International Conflict: Soviet Perceptions of the U.S. and the U.S.S.R." appeared in a recently published volume, *International Behavior*.

it has not "willed" this war. On each side ordinary human beings have become gradually entangled, hating the war and all the suffering associated with it, honestly believing that their manhood requires them to resist the "aggression" of the enemy. But the enemy's "aggression," in the sense in which it has been assumed to exist, has not existed.[1]

For reasons that will be discussed, it follows that the only honorable peace would be a compromise peace in which each side could feel it had held out against the aggressor's onslaught and had managed to preserve at least the bare essentials of what it was fighting to defend.

Can They Believe It When They Call Us "Aggressors"?

President Johnson has said, "The first reality is that North Vietnam has attacked the independent nation of South Vietnam. Its object is total conquest. . . . Let no one think for a moment that retreat from Vietnam would bring an end to the conflict. The battle would be renewed in one country and then another. The central lesson of our time is that the appetite of aggression is never satisfied."[2] Secretary McNamara has said, "The prime aggressor is North Vietnam."[3] Secretary Rusk has repeatedly declared that the whole purpose of our intervention would disappear the moment the North Vietnamese decided to "let their neighbors alone."

The great majority of the American people do not seriously doubt these statements; even among those who doubt the wisdom of our attempting to resist aggression in Southeast Asia there are many who do not doubt that Communist aggression has occurred. Those who do feel that it is our responsibility to resist the aggression that they regard as self-evident are likely to have ready answers to what they suppose to be the arguments against this belief. They may ask: "Can you deny that North Vietnam has sent troops and weapons to the South? Can you deny that the Viet Cong cadres are Communists, controlled by other Communists in Hanoi and perhaps in Peking? Can you deny that war by assassination in the villages is aggression, in principle, as much as is war by invasion of troops across a border?" And when they find that their opponents, while making certain qualifications (e.g., with regard to the completeness of the control of the Viet Cong by Hanoi), do not try to deny the essential truth of any of these

[1] A much more detailed and documented presentation of this thesis is contained in Ralph K. White, "Misperception and the Vietnam War," *Journal of Social Issues*, Vol. XXII, No. 3 (1966), pp. 1-167.

[2] Johns Hopkins speech, Apr. 7, 1965.

[3] Speech before the National Security Industrial Assn., Mar. 26, 1964.

things, they are likely to feel that their case is well established and that Communist aggression is indeed self-evident.

A visitor from Mars would be struck by the close parallel between all of this and the attitudes that are continually expressed on the other side. According to Ho Chi Minh, "It is crystal clear that the United States is the aggressor who is trampling under foot the Vietnamese soil."[4] According to Chou En-lai, "America is rapidly escalating the war in an attempt to subdue the Vietnamese people by armed force."[5] And according to Leonid Brezhnev, "Normalization of our relations [with the U.S.] is incompatible with the armed aggression of American imperialism against a fraternal Socialist country—Vietnam."[6] To the extent that they mean what they say, aggression by us seems as obvious to them as aggression by them seems to us.

That, then, is the essential question: to what extent do they mean what they say?

To most Americans, probably, the charge that *we* are aggressors seems like outrageous nonsense, so transparently false that honest men all over the world must put it down immediately as a propaganda trick by the Communists to cover up their own aggression. The thief is crying "Stop thief!" and must be doing it simply to distract attention from his own crime.

It is precisely here, though, that the perceptions of most Americans are, in my judgment, basically mistaken. The charge that we have been aggressors—inadvertent aggressors, without for a moment intending to be—is not outrageous nonsense. It is no more false than our charge that the Communists have been aggressors. Both charges are psychologically false, since neither side has committed conscious, deliberate, Hitler-like aggression. But both charges are in a less essential sense true, since both sides, in the belief that they have been defending themselves, have engaged in certain actions which the other side, seeing them within a radically different frame of reference, could easily perceive as aggressive.

That this is true on the American side needs no demonstration. Certain actions of the Communists, notably the campaign of assassination in the villages and the sending of troops from the North to the South, have seemed to most Americans, interpreting them within an American frame of refer-

[4] Interview with Felix Greene, quoted in *The Washington Post*, Dec. 14, 1965, pp. A 1, A 16.
[5] Speech in Peking, reported in *The New York Times*, May 1, 1966, p. 4.
[6] Speech to the Central Committee of the CPSU, reported in *The Washington Post*, Sept. 30, 1965, A 16.

ence, to be flagrantly, self-evidently aggressive. What most Americans have almost wholly failed to realize is that we too have done things which, when perceived within the Communists' radically different frame of reference, have probably seemed to them to be just as flagrantly and self-evidently aggressive. This failure to see how our own actions are perceived by the Communists is the essence of our misperception.

Most of the rest of this article will be devoted to an exploration of the reasons for believing that the Communists do see our behavior as aggressive. The argument is twofold. (1) There are at least eight important kernels of truth in the Communist case against us—eight types of evidence that, when strongly focused upon by a Communist mind and interpreted within a Communist frame of reference, could seem to substantiate his charge of American aggression. (2) There is ample reason to believe that the lenses through which the Communists see reality have a high enough degree of refraction to do the rest of the job. They are quite capable of focusing strongly on these kernels of truth, interpreting them solely within a Communist frame of reference, failing to realize that we see them within a quite different frame of reference, ignoring or misinterpreting all the kernels of truth on our side, and therefore coming up with a black-and-white picture in which their role is wholly defensive and ours is aggressive. The chief reason to think they are capable of this much distortion lies in the fact that most American minds—presumably less dogmatic, more evidence-oriented—have been capable of a similar degree of distortion in the opposite direction. The very fact that so many Americans have denied, misinterpreted, soft-pedaled or simply ignored these eight important kernels of truth on the Communist side is sufficient evidence that the capacity to misperceive in this way is not inherently Communist. It is human. In other situations the Communists have, on the whole, shown much more of it than we have, but in the case of Vietnam the amount of distortion that apparently exists in Communist minds, i.e., the amount of it that they would need in order to believe most of what they say, is no greater than the amount in the minds of most Americans.

What is needed, then, is a careful examination of the "eight kernels of truth." We can hardly understand either the sincerity of Communist thinking or the distortions and blind spots in our own until we focus steadily on the facts that to them seem decisively important.

Three Reasons Why They Think South Vietnam "Belongs" to Them

The usage of the term "aggression" in the Communists' discourse suggests that in their minds, as in ours, it is applied when either or both of two conditions exist: (1) when they believe, rightly or wrongly, that country A is using force to take land that "belongs" to country B; and (2) when they believe, rightly or wrongly, that most of the people on that land want to be part of country B. The "eight kernels of truth" mentioned above include three types of evidence that, in my judgment, actually do tend to support their claim that South Vietnam "belongs" to them (reasons other than the belief that the people are on their side) and five types of evidence supporting their claim that most of the people are on their side.

Perhaps it should be repeated: this is not an argument that South Vietnam *does* "belong" to them, or that most of the people *are* on their side. It seems to me that the first of these propositions, when closely analyzed, is largely meaningless, and that the second, though very meaningful, cannot be clearly answered on an empirical basis and is probably somewhat less than half true, since most people in South Vietnam probably do not want to be ruled either by Hanoi or by Saigon. This is simply an argument that the facts are complex and ambiguous enough to disprove completely our prevailing American assumption that there has been deliberate, unequivocal Communist aggression, and to make it highly probable that the Communists *think* South Vietnam belongs to them and the people are on their side.[7]

What does "belonging" mean, psychologically? On what grounds does any group come to feel that a certain piece of land obviously "belongs" to it and not to someone else? Though at first glance the concept seems simple, on closer examination it turns out to be extraordinarily complex and elusive. Such an examination is needed, too, in view of the fact that an endless amount of bad blood and of violent conflict has been generated at the places in the world where two or more groups have had conflicting assumptions about what belongs to whom: the Thirteen Colonies, the Confederate States, Cuba, Bosnia-Herzegovina, Alsace-Lorraine, Austria, the Sudetenland, the Polish Corridor, Danzig, the Baltic states, Taiwan, Quemoy, Tibet, the Sino-Indian border, Indochina, Algeria, Kashmir, Cyprus, Israel. When the territorial self-image of one country overlaps with the territorial self-image of another, trouble seems to be almost inevitable, and such overlapping is hard to avoid because nations differ in their criteria of what constitutes ownership or "belonging." Sometimes, as in our American feeling about the Revolutionary War and the Southern feeling about the Civil War, the criterion is a belief about what most of the

---

[7] For a more balanced picture of the evidence on both sides, see White, *op. cit.*, especially pp. 19-44, 46-50, 89-90, and 106-16.

people in the area want. Sometimes, as in the British feeling about our Revolutionary War and the Northern feeling about the Civil War, it is a compound of habit, respect for tradition and legality, national pride, beliefs (which may be very deeply held) about what is best for all concerned, including minority groups such as the slaves in the American South or the Catholics in South Vietnam, and perhaps anxiety about what may happen elsewhere if violent attacks on the legally established order are allowed to succeed. There is always a tendency to accept whatever definition of "belonging" makes a given piece of land clearly belong to one's own nation or to an ally.

If we ask ourselves why most Americans assume that South Vietnam belongs to the Saigon Government and does not belong to the Viet Cong or to the Communist Government in the North, perhaps the best single answer would be that since 1954 we have regarded this as an established, accepted fact. Since 1954 we have had a mental image of Vietnam as having been divided, as Korea was, between a Communist North and a southern portion that was still part of the free world—perhaps precariously so, but for that reason all the more in need of being shored up and defended. Probably in the minds of most well-informed Americans there has been no belief that most of the people in South Vietnam want the kind of government they have had in Saigon. On that score there have been embarrassing doubts. But the doubts have usually been fairly well resolved in various ways, e.g., by the belief that most of the people in South Vietnam belong to a large, politically apathetic middle group that only wants peace and would gladly go along with whichever side seems likely to be the winner —from which many infer that there is no popular will which needs to be considered, and that we are therefore free to decide the matter on other grounds. Or the doubts may be resolved by the belief that in the long run a government sponsored by us would permit a genuine development of democracy and national independence, whereas no Communist government would do so; or by the belief that permitting a Communist use of force to succeed in South Vietnam would encourage the "wars of liberation" favored by Communist China and therefore endanger both peace and freedom throughout the world. But all of these points also encounter controversy, and when tired of such controversy many Americans, including Dean Rusk, fall back on the solid, simple, and (they feel) unanswerable proposition that there are Communist soldiers fighting on land that does not "belong" to them. "We will stay until they decide to let their neighbors alone." And the seeming obviousness of this "belonging," since it cannot be based on assumptions about what the people want, is probably based primarily on the fact that for at least twelve years there has been, on our maps and in our minds, a division between the Communist North and the non-Communist South. We see this as the established, accepted, natural order of things.

In doing so we ignore three facts that in Communist minds are much more important than the division of the country that occurred in 1954.

1. *The division of the country has its only legal basis in the Geneva Conference of 1954, and at that conference it was explicitly agreed that it would last only two years.* The Communist-led Viet Minh stopped fighting on the basis of what seemed to be a firm agreement that there would be an all-Vietnamese vote in 1956 (which they fully expected to win) that would unify the country, establishing both unity and full independence without further bloodshed. According to the respected French historian Philippe Devillers, "The demarcation line was to be purely provisional; the principle of Vietnamese unity was not questioned, and the idea of partition was officially rejected with indignation by both sides. When military forces were regrouped and administrative divisions laid down, national unity would be restored by free general elections."[8]

Informed Americans are now embarrassingly aware (though a great many reasonably well-informed Americans were not clearly aware of it until perhaps two or three years ago) that in 1956 Diem, apparently with American backing, refused to permit the elections that had been provided for by the Geneva Agreement. To be sure, neither he nor we had signed those agreements, and there were other persuasive reasons for not permitting the elections at that time or at any time since then. But that is not the present point at issue; the point is that, having in effect rejected the Geneva Agreement by not carrying out one of its key provisions, Diem and the United States deprived themselves of any right to invoke the Geneva Agreement as a legal or moral sanction for the division of the country. With Diem's decision not to press for a plebiscite under international supervision even in "his own" southern part of the country, he forfeited—at least in Communist eyes—not only all claim to the kind of legitimacy that genuine popular endorsement would have provided, but also all claim to invoke the Geneva Conference's endorsement of the 17th Parallel as a basis for his own rule in the South. In effect he proclaimed *de facto* control— "possession is nine-tenths of the law"—as his sole basis of legitimacy.

In the same year—and this is a fact that very few Americans know,

[8] Philippe Devillers, "The Struggle for Unification of Vietnam," *China Quarterly*, No. 9 (1962), pp. 2-23.

though it is of great importance to the villagers in South Vietnam who became members of the Viet Cong—Diem abolished the fine old semi-democratic Vietnamese system of electing village councils and mayors, which had survived even during the period of French rule. Both of these actions by Diem must have seemed to the Communists to be flagrantly anti-democratic, anti-Vietnamese, and a violation of the agreement on the basis of which they had laid down their arms. It was only *after* both had occurred, in 1957, that the Viet Cong began their campaign of assassination of government-appointed officials in the villages. From their standpoint, the decisive acts of armed aggression against them occurred in 1956, and anything they have done since then has only been defensive.

2. *In the years between 1950 and 1954, when the United States was supplying money and arms on a large scale to the French, the French were fighting against a clear majority of the Vietnamese people.*

The years before 1954 represent another major blind spot in the thinking of most Americans, though they are probably ever present in the thinking of the Vietnamese Communists. For them those years were as terrible and as heroic as the years of World War II were for the Communists in the Soviet Union.

Few Americans realize that in 1945 and 1946, when the postwar world was settling down to its present division between East and West, Vietnam was not so divided. Instead, it was enjoying the first flush of what seemed to be independence from the rule of France, under Ho Chi Minh's leadership. Since he was a Communist, this meant that the boundary between the two worlds was at that time the boundary of Vietnam itself. Vietnam as a whole had in a sense "gone Communist" when it accepted Ho's leadership. It was, then, the West that stepped over the boundary and used force on the far side of it. France began then, and continued until 1954—with massive American financial help after 1950—to try to reimpose her rule. Although there was talk of a new autonomous role for the three states of Indochina within the French Union, the anti-French majority of the Vietnamese could be forgiven for regarding this war as naked aggression on the part of France, aided greatly by the United States. The term "imperialist," which sounds so strange in American ears when applied to ourselves, does not sound so strange in the ears of Vietnamese who regarded French rule as imperialist and had much reason to associate alien intruding Frenchmen with alien intruding Americans. As for the word "aggressor," it is difficult to escape the conclusion that, by any definition of the term, we were committing aggression in Vietnam from 1950 to 1954. We were financing the use of force on land that did not "belong" to us—or to the

French—by any criterion that we would now accept, and we were doing it against what now clearly seems to have been a majority of the people.

On this last point we have the testimony of many people, including President Eisenhower. As he put it in a much-quoted passage, "I have never talked or corresponded with a person knowledgeable in Indochinese affairs who did not agree that had elections been held as of the time of the fighting, possibly 80 per cent of the populace would have voted for the Communist Ho Chi Minh as their leader rather than Chief of State Bao Dai."[9]

Since President Eisenhower's statement has often been misinterpreted it should be noted that he did not say that Ho Chi Minh would probably have won by 80 per cent in the elections that Diem refused to hold in 1956. He said "possibly;" he carefully said "had elections been held as of the time of the fighting," i.e., in 1954 or earlier, not in 1956, when Diem's prospect of victory would have been much brighter; and he specified as Ho's hypothetical opponent Bao Dai, who was generally regarded as a weak French stooge, rather than Diem, who at that time was regarded even by many of his enemies as an honest man and a staunch anti-French patriot. But on the point that is now at issue—whether the help we gave to the French was in effect a use of force against a majority of the Vietnamese people—President Eisenhower's statement would seem to be decisive.

Why did we do it? Our reasons were understandable if not valid. In 1950 the Communists had just won in China; they were starting the Korean war, and it looked as if desperate measures were necessary in order to keep all of East and Southeast Asia from succumbing to the Communist juggernaut. Perhaps President Truman was honest enough to say to himself that even aggression against the Vietnamese was justified by the magnitude of the emergency. If present-day Americans are able to be equally honest and to remember clearly the situation as it was then, it will help them to understand how present-day Vietnamese Communists could really regard us as aggressors.

3. *The Communist-led majority of the Vietnamese people had actually won their war for independence in 1954.*

Though they were supported to some extent by arms from China, the arms their enemies gained from the United States and from France were far more formidable. Consequently, one of the clearest indications that a large majority of the Vietnamese people did support Ho lies in the fact

[9] Dwight D. Eisenhower, *Mandate for Change* (Garden City, N.Y.: Doubleday and Co., Inc., 1963), p. 372.

that his ragged, relatively poorly armed troops did finally win. The battle of Dienbienphu was decisive, and it was generally agreed at the time that if the Viet Minh had wanted to fight a few months more they could have had the whole country.

This is an important part of the psychological background of the Geneva Agreements, and of everything that has happened since. In this respect the situation was very different from the situation in Korea in 1945, when the boundary at the 38th Parallel was first established, or in Korea in 1953, when a military stalemate finally led to a new and roughly similar truce line. In 1953 there was a military stalemate in Korea and the Communists had no basis at all for setting their hearts on unifying the country on their terms. In Vietnam they did. The Vietnamese Communists and the many non-Communists who fought with them had every reason to feel that the prize for which they had struggled and sacrificed through nine heartbreaking years of war was finally theirs: a unified, independent country. Then, by what must have seemed to them a form of chicanery, with the face of America appearing where the face of France had been, and with both Diem and John Foster Dulles blandly claiming that they were not bound by the decisions made at Geneva, a full half of the prize they felt they had fairly won was snatched from them.

Apart from any question of what the people want, then, the Vietnamese Communists have three additional reasons for feeling that South Vietnam "belongs" to them and not to the government established and maintained by us in Saigon: the artificial division of the country at the 17th Parallel was legally and morally invalid after 1956; their war for independence was supported by a large majority of the people; they won that war.

Five Reasons Why They Think the People of South Vietnam Are on Their Side

Since Communists have repeatedly said that any people has a right to fight a "war of liberation" against colonial overlords, no matter how much the rule of the overlords may be sanctioned by tradition and legality, it is clear that their decisive criterion of "aggression" (if they are consistent with their official statements) must be whether "the people" oppose it or not. The following five types of evidence, of which they are probably much more aware than the average American, are therefore relevant to the question of their sincerity on this point.

1. *There are many reasons to think that Vietnamese nationalism is now mobilized, and has been mobilized for some twenty years, much more in*

favor of Ho Chi Minh than in favor of the French-backed or American-backed government in Saigon.

In Vietnam, perhaps more than in any other developing country, the Communists have apparently succeeded in fusing Communism with nationalism, and especially with the cause of national unity. The long and finally victorious struggle against the French was conducted primarily under Communist leadership by peasants who regarded their leaders more as patriots than as Communists.[10] President Eisenhower's statement, quoted above, is very relevant here.[11]

It should be noted too that the more and more conspicuous role of America on the Saigon Government side since 1960 has been such as to mobilize the xenophobic nationalism of the Vietnamese in a new way. Since 1960 American aid to Saigon has become far greater and more obvious, while Chinese aid to the Communists has been on a much smaller scale. There are many big-nosed white faces now on the Government side of the war, while those on the Viet Cong side are authentically Vietnamese, even though now a considerable and very potent fraction of them have come down from the North. The Viet Cong guerrillas have been helped by their own countrymen, while the Government has incurred what is probably a much greater stigma by accepting massive help from white foreigners who cannot even speak Vietnamese.

2. *The peasants want land, and many of them have had land taken away from them by the Government.*

Although there is a village-centered peasant nationalism, it may well be that another motive—hunger—is even more basic in the typical peasant's make-up. He wants to safeguard the bowl of rice that represents his next meal, and the rice field that represents next year's meals for himself, his wife, and his children. From the standpoint of many peasants in the southern part of South Vietnam, especially the Mekong Delta, their rice and their rice fields have been under attack not only by the crop-destroying chemicals that have been dropped (in some areas) by Government planes, but also by the absentee landlords who have in many instances demanded between thirty and fifty per cent of the crop. This fact of absentee landlordism in the

[10] Bernard Fall, *The Two Vietnams* (New York: Frederick A. Praeger, 1964), pp. 104-29; Ellen Hammer, *The Struggle for Indochina* (Stanford: Stanford University Press, 1954); Jean Lacouture, *Vietnam Between Two Truces* (New York: Random House, 1966), pp. 5, 8, and 32.

[11] On the importance and nature of Vietnamese nationalism, see George A. Carver, Jr., "The Real Revolution in South Viet Nam," *Foreign Affairs*, Vol. XLIII, No. 3 (1965), especially pp. 399 and 403.

Misperception of Aggression in Vietnam

South is little known in the United States. It has been estimated that in South Vietnam proper (Cochin China, roughly the southern one-third of the country) only two per cent of the people owned forty-five per cent of the land before 1945.[12] Land reform since then has not greatly changed the situation. Some has occurred under Diem and his successors, but it was preceded by a drastic reclaiming of land that the Viet Minh, when it was in control of large areas in South Vietnam, had given to the peasants outright. Land reform by the present government has been a pale imitation of land reform under the Communist-led Viet Minh.

3. *Probably much more physical suffering has been imposed on the peasants by the Government and its American allies than by the Viet Cong.*

On this point Americans have had misperceptions of two quite different kinds. On the one hand there is the misperception of those Americans who, shocked by occasional television pictures of weeping mothers, roughly handled prisoners, and deliberately burned villages, have failed to realize that the atrocities of the Viet Cong, less accessible to Western photographers and less vividly depicted, are just as real. Public disembowelment of "enemies of the people" and of their wives and children is only one of the revolting procedures employed by them, and it has seldom found its way to our American newspaper pages or television screens. On the other hand, there is the misperception of those Americans who, focusing primarily on the widely discussed Viet Cong assassinations of teachers, health workers, and Government-appointed village officials, have often remained ignorant of the highly probable fact that, because of the nature of guerrilla and counter-guerrilla war, the sheer volume of suffering inflicted by the Government has been considerably greater than that inflicted by the Viet Cong.

There are two reasons for this. The more familiar one is that the present process of using American firepower and mobility to break the back of the Viet Cong has meant—despite genuine efforts to minimize it—a large amount of killing, maiming, and sometimes napalming of villagers who, whether "innocent" from our point of view or not, certainly regard themselves as innocent.[13] In a culture that values family loyalty as much as the Vietnamese culture does, this deeply affects not only those who have suffered from it themselves but also those who have seen a parent or other relative suffer or die.

The less familiar reason for it is that, in the conduct of counter-guerrilla

[12] Fall, *op. cit.*, pp. 308-11.
[13] Major-General Edward G. Lansdale, "Viet Nam: Do We Understand Revolution?" *Foreign Affairs*, Vol. XLIII, No. 1 (1964), p. 81.

operations, it is urgently necessary to obtain intelligence about the identity of the guerrilla fighters and where they are hiding. South Vietnamese soldiers have interpreted this as justifying a large-scale use of torture to obtain information not only from captured Viet Cong prisoners themselves but also from wives and relatives of men suspected of being in the Viet Cong. There is the water torture, the electric-current torture, the wire-cage torture—all widely used—and there are other kinds even less well-known in the United States (perhaps chiefly because of unofficial self-censorship by most of our information gatherers in Saigon) but well documented by observers such as Bernard Fall, Malcolm Browne, and Robin Moore.[14]

The ignorance and apathy of the great majority of the American public with regard to this ugliest aspect of the war represent in themselves a puzzling and very disturbing psychological phenomenon. Bernard Fall in 1965 spoke about "the universally callous attitude taken by almost everybody toward the crass and constant violations of the rules of war that have been taking place . . . . To me the moral problem which arises in Vietnam is that of torture and needless brutality to combatants and civilians alike."[15] But the fact of widely used torture has not been cited here as an accusation against the United States. As we have seen, some of the Viet Cong atrocities have been at least as bad. The direct participants in the torture have as a rule been South Vietnamese, not Americans, and during the past year (partly as a result of the article by Bernard Fall quoted above) the American military authorities have provided American troops with clear instructions not only as to the applicability of the 1949 Convention on the humane treatment of prisoners but also as to the long-run counterproductive character of the torturing of prisoners and their relatives. The fact is cited here because it provides such an emotionally compelling kernel of truth in the Communist case against the Saigon Government, as well as for the Communist thesis that the common people *must* hate that government. Simply by focusing on this and ignoring similar atrocities on the Communist side a Communist could arrive at that conclusion.

4. *There has been a great deal of inefficiency and corruption on the part of the local officials appointed by the Saigon Government.*

The tradition of exploitation and cheating of the peasants by Government-appointed officials is perhaps no worse than in a number of other

[14] Bernard Fall, "Vietnam Blitz: A Report on the Impersonal War," *The New Republic*, Oct. 9, 1965, pp. 18-21; Malcolm W. Browne, *The New Face of War* (New York: Bobbs-Merrill, 1965), pp. 114-18; Robin Moore, *The Green Berets* (New York: Avon Books, 1965), pp. 46-50.

[15] Fall, *ibid.*, pp. 19-20.

Asian countries, including pre-Communist China; but it is very bad,[16] and it does contrast with the Viet Cong's tradition of comparative honesty and concern with the welfare of the rank-and-file peasants.[17] Inefficiency is also clearly very common, in contrast with the quite extraordinary efficiency (in some ways) of the Viet Cong; and in many relatively inaccessible villages the choice is not between the Viet Cong type of village government and that of the Saigon officials, but between Viet Cong government and virtually no government at all. In these villages the Viet Cong cadres fill a political vacuum and provide an alternative to anarchy. To be sure, they themselves have helped to produce the anarchy by assassinating Government-appointed village leaders. But their tactics have not been the only cause of anarchy, and they themselves are probably more aware, indeed inordinately aware, of their own comparative honesty and efficiency, which "must" bring the peasants over to their side.

None of this, it may be noted, is incompatible with the fact, now well documented, that in the years since 1963 the Viet Cong's high-handed methods of taxation and recruitment among the peasants have become more and more burdensome. The comparative honesty and efficiency of Viet Cong functionaries are linked with an essentially authoritarian attitude and a willingness to subordinate peasant welfare to the progress of the war. But *in their minds* the peasant's resentment of such tactics is probably underestimated, while his appreciation of their more positive contributions is probably overestimated.

5. *The Viet Cong has a record of remarkable military success against enormous obstacles, and it seems unlikely that such success could have been achieved without widespread popular support.*

Americans sometimes forget or underestimate the great advantage that the anti-Communist forces have enjoyed from the standpoint of weapons, especially since America began in 1950 to give large-scale material help to the French. The total amount of such help has clearly been much greater than the material help the Viet Cong has received from the North. Moreover, few Americans realize that the rebellion did not begin in the part of South Vietnam near Laos and the Ho Chi Minh Trail, where an appreciable amount of help from the North might have been possible. It began primarily in the far South, in the Mekong Delta, where it was necessary to use mainly homemade or captured weapons. The rebels therefore had to

---

[16] M. Mok, "In They Go—To the Reality of This War," *Life*, Nov. 26, 1965, p. 71.

[17] Malcolm Browne, *op. cit.*, pp. 121-28; Viet Cong Soldiers' Diaries, quoted in *The Vietnam Reader*, ed. by M. G. Raskin and Bernard Fall (New York: Random House, 1965), p. 227.

make up in organization, dedication, and extent of popular support for the Government's great advantage in material equipment.[18] Still another fact frequently forgotten in America (or never learned) is that the rebellion began to a significant extent in 1957,[19] at least three years before its surprising success—with little outside help—led the Communist authorities in the North to give it a significant amount of material help.

It is true that one major compensating advantage possessed by the Viet Cong has been the tactical advantage of concealment and surprise that has led to the conventional estimate that counter-guerrilla forces must have a ten-to-one numerical superiority over guerrilla forces in order to defeat them. But what is sometimes forgotten is that the guerrillas' tactical advantage exists to this high degree only when they have the active support of most of the people (which they could hardly get by intimidation alone) in helping them to conceal themselves, in helping to supply them with the intelligence they need in order to have the full advantage of surprise, and in denying to the counter-guerrilla forces the same kind of intelligence.

Here too there are important counterarguments on the anti-Communist side. In particular the use of intimidation by the Viet Cong to clinch their hold on the peasants must account for much of the peasant cooperation that has occurred. But here again it is important to note that the Communists themselves are probably overinclined to discount or ignore those counterarguments. The military successes of the Viet Cong against far better armed opponents have been remarkable enough to enable Communists to say to themselves: "The people *must* be on our side."

* * * *

There are at least five reasons, then, to think that the Communists believe most of the people are on their side: nationalistic resentment of intrusion by white Americans, land hunger, resentment of torture and other physical suffering caused by the Government, the corruption of officials, and the military success of the Viet Cong against great material odds.

Together with the three additional reasons reviewed earlier for thinking they feel that South Vietnam is part of "their" country, these five seem quite adequate to make it probable that doctrinaire Communists, already predisposed against the United States, do believe it when they call us "aggressors." However mistaken this proposition may be (and I happen to

---

[18] Fall, *The Two Vietnams*, p. 317; Lacouture, *op. cit.*, pp. 21-23.
[19] Carver, *op. cit.*, p. 406.

think it is largely mistaken, on the basis of evidence that has hardly been touched upon here), the Communists probably *believe* it is true.[20]

A Sensible and Honorable Compromise

The preceding discussion is a diagnosis of the problem, not a prescription for its solution. In the light of this diagnosis, though, my own feeling is that the most sensible and honorable policy for the United States is to seek a compromise peace. It is the only kind of peace that would allow *both* sides to feel that they had preserved from the aggressor's grasp the bare essentials of what they were fighting to defend.

It could take various forms. One is a coalition government, with efforts by other countries to keep the coalition from being dominated by the organized, dedicated Communist minority within it. Such a coalition could be the outcome of negotiations, if genuine negotiations become possible, or it might conceivably be set up by our side unilaterally, with a real effort to give the Viet Cong and all other elements of the population power commensurate with their actual strength. Or it could take the form of a partition of the South along lines reflecting the balance of military power at the time the partition occurs. This too could be done with negotiations if possible but without negotiations if necessary—unilaterally, by a decision to concentrate our military strength on consolidating non-Communist control of large contiguous areas (not small "enclaves") while withdrawing from overexposed, hard-to-hold areas elsewhere. Free migration into and out of each area might follow, as it did in the partition that followed the 1954 agreement.

As to the relative merits of different types of compromise peace there are complex pro's and con's, and this is not the place to discuss them. What is argued here is that a search for *some* feasible form of compromise peace is the only sensible and honorable policy for the United States.

When each side believes the other to be the aggressor, both are sure to regard any compromise as unsatisfactory, since each will see a compromise as granting to the aggressor some part of his ill-gotten gains. Each wants to ensure that the aggressor is not rewarded by any expansion whatsoever. In this case, for instance, we Americans and our Vietnamese allies would hate to accept a compromise that we defined as granting to the Communists any expansion of power, either by gaining some land south of the

---

[20] Douglas Pike, *Viet Cong* (Cambridge, Mass.: M.I.T. Press, 1966), p. 378. Although Pike is very skeptical of the proposition that most of the people support the Viet Cong, he speaks of the party's "mystic belief in the power *and loyalty* of the people." Italics added.

17th Parallel or by gaining some power in a coalition government. The Communists would similarly regard with dismay a compromise peace that left the American "aggressors" still firmly ensconced on Vietnamese soil and still (as they would see it) ruling a large part of the country through their lackeys in Saigon. To them it would seem like a bitter and futile end to their twenty years of struggle to drive the alien white intruders into the sea.

As long as both sides rigidly adhere to this principle, a compromise is clearly impossible. However, *if* there is no clear break in the present military stalemate and the bloody, inhuman war continues with no end in sight, each side may lower its sights and begin to consider seriously whether some form of compromise would necessarily be cowardly and dishonorable. Probably both sides would even then be grimly determined never to surrender. "Surrender is unthinkable." But each side might become aware that it had a hierarchy of preferences. Three choices might emerge instead of only two: surrender (unthinkable), a compromise peace, and unending war, instead of surrender (unthinkable) and victory. Among these three choices a compromise peace might then seem the least intolerable.

What are the bare essentials of what each side is fighting to defend? Are they incompatible? Or would it be possible for both sides simultaneously to preserve what they care about most?

On our side, it seems to me, there are two things that a large majority of the American people regard as essential: to avoid a significant "domino" process in other parts of the world, and to preserve a tolerable life for our anti-Communist friends in Vietnam. The first of these is believed to be a matter of defending both freedom and peace: the freedom of other countries that are vulnerable to the Chinese strategy of takeover by "wars of liberation," and the peace that would be endangered elsewhere if a Communist victory in Vietnam led Communists everywhere to be more aggressive. The second is more a matter of honor and commitment. We feel that our words and actions have established a commitment to our anti-Communist allies, and that if we abandoned them to the untender mercies of the Viet Cong we would be doing a shameful thing. The validity of these two points will not be debated here; it is necessary only to recognize that most of the Americans who would be involved in the decision do care about both of them, and care deeply.

On the Communist side there are as yet no verbal indications of a hierarchy of preferences. On the surface there is only a fervent, monolithic insistence that the American aggressors must be wholly eliminated from the scene; and since we feel that any complete withdrawal by us would both accentuate the domino process and leave our anti-Communist friends helpless in the face of the organized, dedicated, vengeful Viet Cong, there is little chance of a compromise on this basis. It seems likely, though, that beneath the surface they do have a hierarchy of preferences. Perhaps, if convinced that the alternative is not victory but unending war, they would prefer peace with undisturbed control of some large fraction (say a half) of the population of South Vietnam. This would mean that they could stay alive, go back to the increasingly urgent business of cultivating their rice paddies, and preserve the way of life in which they have invested so much effort and sacrifice. The Communists in the North would be spared further bombing and the danger of a wider war, and although they would have failed in their great objective of unifying the country under their own control, they could salvage some pride in the thought that they had held their own against a much more powerful aggressor.

On each side, then, a compromise peace might be interpreted as salvaging the bare essentials of what that side was fighting to defend. It therefore seems psychologically feasible if we pursue it intelligently and persistently.

It also seems more honorable than any other alternative. By keeping the American flag flying in South Vietnam and stubbornly refusing to retreat from our present power position we would be balancing the power of Communist China on its periphery and fulfilling our obligation to the small non-Communist countries that are threatened by Communist takeover. We would also be fulfilling our obligation to preserve the life and livelihood of our non-Communist friends in Vietnam itself. But if we attempted by force of arms to conquer the parts of South Vietnam in which most of the people regard us as alien aggressors—and the evidence suggests that a very large proportion of the people in certain areas see us in that light—we would be in conflict with the principle of self-determination. It is not in the American tradition to impose abject surrender on brave men who believe, rightly or wrongly, that they are defending their homeland against aggression by us.